FROM THE HOUSE & GARDENS AT

Cranbrook

George Booth's Cranbrook bookplate adapted from library mantel.

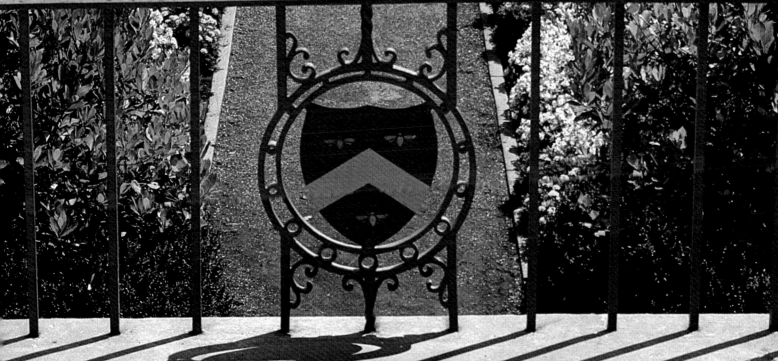

"We hope
bees are
appropriate
symbols
for they
not only seek
what is beautiful,
sweet,
and nourishing
but make enough
honey to satisfy
the needs of
many others as well
as their own."

HENRY S. BOOTH

Cranbrook House & Gardens Auxiliary is a
volunteer organization dedicated to the restoration
and preservation of the historically significant estate
home and gardens of George Gough and Ellen
Scripps Booth. The house and gardens provide a
place of enjoyment for the public through tours,
special events and community gatherings. Proceeds
realized from the sale of CRANBROOK REFLECTIONS
will go to continue the work of the Auxiliary.

For further information regarding tours write to
Cranbrook House & Gardens,
380 Lone Pine Road, Box 801, Bloomfield Hills,
Michigan 48303-0801 or call 313-645-3149

Printed on recycled paper

Library of Contress Catalog Card Number
90-86326

ISBN 0-9628714-0-0

Printed in the USA by Wimmer Brothers

Design:
Mary Lou Kroh

Photography:
Balthazar Korab

# CRANBROOK

## REFLECTIONS

**A CULINARY COLLECTION**

Cranbrook House & Gardens Auxiliary    Bloomfield Hills, Michigan

# The Committee

| | |
|---|---|
| *Chairman* | Susie L. Andersen |
| *Food Editor* | Geri Rinschler |
| *Copy Editor* | Judith Miller |
| *Computer Services* | Christine Cameron |
| *Committee* | Roslyn L. Basherian |
| | Tirzah Anne Cunningham |
| | Irene Davis |
| | Elaine Drane |
| | Lois Gamble |
| | Betty Kneen |
| | Judy Lindstrom |
| | Rita Lindstrom |
| | Rita Mason |
| | Phyllis McLean |
| | Martha Neumann |
| | Olga Omelianoff |
| | Shirley Park |
| | By Parrott |
| | Jerry Risk |
| | Kathleen Sheean |
| | Hildegard Stanley |
| | Phyllis Twinney |

Sunken Garden in spri

# FOREWORD

Designated a National Historic Landmark in 1989, Cranbrook Educational Community receives visitors in the hundreds of thousands each year. Many of our visitors come to see Cranbrook House and Gardens that are maintained with great care and affection by hundreds of volunteers who are members of our distinguished Cranbrook House and Gardens Auxiliary.

Auxiliary members have played a key role in the restoration of the Booth estate home. Largely as a result of their dedication to excellence, the home today reflects the warm, family atmosphere of the Booths while displaying well its preserved works of art.

Cranbrook's gardens are extraordinarily beautiful in each season of the year. Auxiliary members plant flowers and foliage with considerable creativity. The design and pattern of their work results in an ever-changing array of color and texture that is a wonder to see.

The women and men who care for Cranbrook House and Gardens are motivated by their love of Cranbrook. We are deeply appreciative of their efforts and proud that they are members of our Cranbrook family, for they are among the finest volunteers anywhere in America.

Cranbrook House and Gardens Auxiliary's creation of this cookbook continues a Booth tradition that combines and celebrates food and fellowship. George and Ellen Booth enjoyed inviting guests to their home for Sunday evening dinners in the spacious Oak Room. Through this practice of conviviality, they sustained many friendships and helped to create the human community that is a hallmark of Cranbrook Educational Community.

I hope you find among these recipes many opportunities for good food and fellowship. Bon appétit!

DR. LILLIAN BAUDER, President
Cranbrook Educational Community

Ellen's Garden, Library Terrace

# The History of
# Cranbrook House & Gardens

The Cranbrook story began in 1904 when George Gough Booth, publisher of the Detroit Evening News, and Ellen Scripps Booth purchased a neglected farm in the gently rolling countryside of Bloomfield Hills, north of Detroit. They named it "Cranbrook" after the village in Kent, England from which George's grandfather had emigrated in 1844.

George and Ellen and their five children moved into Cranbrook House, designed by architect Albert Kahn, in the summer of their twenty-first wedding anniversary year, 1908. Landscape architects, gardeners, and laborers transformed the barren land into a beautiful country estate. Thousands of trees were planted, gardens, walks, and waterfalls were built, sculpture and fountains installed, and over the years, imaginative features such as a Greek Theatre and an Italian boathouse were created.

The Booths were leading patrons of the Arts and Crafts Movement in America. They achieved a distinction among owners of American estates by commissioning the finest artisans and craftsmen of the period to embellish the house with outstanding woodcarving, tapestries, oriental rugs, hand-bound books, tile, stained glass, and metalwork.

In their later years, the Booths devoted much of their personal wealth and energy toward the establishment of what is now known as Cranbrook Educational Community, which includes Cranbrook Academy of Art and Museum, Cranbrook Institute of Science, and Cranbrook Schools. The designs for the buildings were primarily the work of the Finnish-American architect, Eliel Saarinen. In addition, the Booths built Christ Church Cranbrook, a magnificent neo-Gothic edifice on Lone Pine Road across from Cranbrook House.

George and Ellen Booth continued to live at Cranbrook until their deaths in 1949 and 1948 respectively. They had, a few years before, donated Cranbrook House, its first floor furnishings, much of its art work, and forty acres of homestead property to the Cranbrook Foundation.

Turtle Fountain, Circular Terrace

By the late 1960's, the gardens surrounding Cranbrook House had become neglected. There was no endowment to defray costs of restoration, maintenance, or plant material and thought was given to tearing down the house and subdividing the property. These were the conditions that led to the formation of the Cranbrook House and Gardens Auxiliary in 1971 by Henry Scripps Booth, youngest son of the Founders.

Now, twenty years later, there are five hundred members of the Auxiliary who continue to share this beautiful oasis with the public. They work diligently to maintain and improve the fifteen theme gardens and the greenhouse which includes an orchid room. A team of volunteers work one step ahead of developers to rescue endangered Michigan wildflowers from various sites around Southeastern Michigan. Restoration of outdoor sculpture and rare antiques contained within the house are ongoing projects of these devoted volunteers.

Each year thousands of visitors from around the world come to Cranbrook House and Gardens to delight in the formal gardens and terraces enhanced by sculpture and fountains. Many enjoy luncheon in the house and tours of both the house and gardens conducted by docents.

Beyond the fieldstone walls are spacious lawns and a lake. Spring brings wildflowers, drifts of daffodils, masses of tulips, and blossoming redbud and dogwood trees. Early summer floral displays include peonies, roses, herb and rock gardens, and perennial borders. Intricate patterns of annuals appear in the Sunken Garden in late summer. Fall offers spectacular vistas of rich changing color and as one garden completes its show there is another to surprise and delight the senses.

The estate is a reflection of a gracious style of living from the early part of this century. It also remains a reflection of George and Ellen Booth themselves and their wide range of interests, personal tastes, and commitment to art, education, and community service.

Cranbrook House Entrance Court

# INTRODUCTION

The recipe collection in this first cookbook by the Cranbrook House and Gardens Auxiliary expresses a renewed interest in classic cooking techniques using fresh ingredients with herbs and spices. Michigan is especially noted for its abundance of apples, cherries, blueberries, asparagus, cucumbers, legumes, and wild morel mushrooms as well as for plentiful game. Recipes designed to feature this regional bounty are found throughout the book.

The creativity of distinguished local restaurant chefs is clearly demonstrated in the favorite recipes they have generously donated in various categories. The Auxiliary's best kept secret, recipes for our noted Michigan navy bean soup mix and fragrant Tussy Mussy potpourri, popular gift items at our annual Fall Plant Sale, are also shared here.

Many more recipes than could possibly be used were submitted by Auxiliary members, friends, and friends of friends. All were appreciated. Volunteers tested and critiqued each one. The final selections which make up Cranbrook Reflections are offered in the hope that you will find them interesting and enjoyable, and that they will enhance your culinary repertoire.

GERI RINSCHLER, Food Editor

# TABLE OF CONTENTS

The Committee                                    4

Foreword                                         6

The History of Cranbrook
House & Gardens                                  8

Introduction                                    12

Appetizers                                      19

Breads                                          35

Soups                                           49

Salads                                          61

Meats                                           75

Poultry & Game                                  91

Fish & Seafood                                 105

Vegetables, Pasta & Rice                       117

Desserts                                       135

Breakfast & Brunch                             153

Herbs & Spices                                 169

Culinary Gifts                                 183

Acknowledgments                                196

Index                                          199

Cranbrook House Dining Room

I lean upon my window sill

And see a golden daffodil;

The more I look, the more I see

And count beyond just one two three

Until the number's up so high

I need a ladder to the sky.

They're like a river down the hill—

The golden River Daffodil.

# APPETIZERS

## BRUSCHETTA

 1   loaf crusty sourdough French bread, unsliced
¼-½  cup virgin olive oil
5-6  large garlic cloves, peeled
 5   medium-size ripe tomatoes, sliced ½ inch thick
 20  large fresh basil leaves

Preheat broiler or barbeque grill. Slice several pieces of bread (½ inch thick) and toast both sides. Remove, brush one side of each slice liberally with olive oil. Rub each slice with a garlic clove, top with tomato slice and a basil leaf. Serve immediately. Continue repeating this process until all ingredients are used.

SERVES 8-10.

**A rustic Italian appetizer that's even better when made over a charcoal grill!**

## APRICOT BRANDIED BRIE

 1   pound round Brie cheese
 1   cup apricot preserves
 6   tablespoons Cognac brandy
 2   tablespoons orange Curaçao liqueur
1½  tablespoons triple sec liqueur
     GARNISH:
     strawberries or grapes
 2   French bread baguette loaves, sliced
     (½ inch thick)

Allow Brie to come to room temperature. Pierce with fork in several places. In saucepan, mix preserves, brandy, and liqueurs over medium heat; remove before boiling. Pour over Brie. Garnish with strawberries and/or grapes. Serve with bread slices.

SERVES 6.

## CURRY CREAM DUNK

½  cup sour cream
½  cup mayonnaise
1  teaspoon grated onion
1  tablespoon prepared horseradish
1  tablespoon vinegar
1  teaspoon seasoned salt
1  tablespoon sugar
1-2  teaspoons curry powder (to taste)
2-3  cups assorted raw vegetables, washed
    and trimmed

Mix together sour cream and mayonnaise; add onion, horseradish, vinegar, and seasonings, blending well. Adjust curry to taste. Refrigerate 2-3 hours. Serve on a tray surrounded by chilled raw vegetables.

SERVES 6.

## MARINATED MUSHROOMS

1  pound fresh mushrooms, rinsed and trimmed
1  medium red onion, sliced thin
½  cup cider or wine vinegar
½  cup olive oil
1  garlic clove, sliced thin
1  tablespoon sugar
1½  teaspoons salt
2  tablespoons water
    dash of pepper
    dash of Tabasco sauce

Toss above ingredients together in a bowl until well mixed. Refrigerate 5-6 hours, stirring occasionally. Before serving remove mushrooms from marinade and serve chilled.

SERVES 6-8.

## SMOKED TROUT PÂTÉ

1 *pound smoked trout, coarsely flaked*
3 *ounces cream cheese, room temperature*
½ *cup half & half*
1 *tablespoon horseradish sauce*
1 *tablespoon fresh lemon juice*
2 *teaspoons chopped parsley*
*fresh ground pepper to taste*

 Place ingredients in a blender and purée until smooth. Remove and spoon into a small serving bowl or crock. Chill 2-3 hours. Serve with crackers, toast points, small canapé bread slices, or on a bed of lettuce as a first course.

SERVES 12.

**A simple, easy prelude to a seafood, poultry, or game dinner.**

## GARLIC ROASTED PEPPERS

2 *large red bell peppers*
1 *cup olive oil, warmed*
12 *cloves garlic, minced*

 Roast peppers using one of two techniques: (1) hold pepper over gas flame, rotating as necessary until skin is blackened and blistered; or (2) trim ends off of pepper and make vertical cuts to form flat strips. Roast under broiler skin side up until blackened and blistered. As soon as skin is blistered, seal in a small paper bag for 5 minutes. Remove and peel. Heat olive oil in a small skillet, and sauté garlic 5-7 minutes until lightly golden. Remove from heat and allow to cool 10 minutes. Slice pepper into one-half-inch strips and set in small container or jar with lid. Pour warm oil and garlic over peppers until covered. Allow to macerate several hours, remove from oil before serving. Serve at room temperature. Peppers will keep several days stored in refrigerator.

SERVES 4-6.

## SWEET AND SOUR MEATBALLS

2   pounds very lean beef, ground fine
2   eggs
¼   cup water
1   cup dried bread crumbs
1   small onion, chopped
    salt and pepper to taste
2   cups jellied cranberry sauce
1½  cups chili sauce
3   tablespoons dark brown sugar
1½  tablespoons fresh lemon juice
    olive oil for browning

In a large mixing bowl, combine beef, eggs, bread crumbs, onion, and salt and pepper and mix thoroughly. Shape into approximately 80 small balls. Heat oil in large skillet and brown meatballs. Remove and drain. Combine cranberry sauce, chili sauce, brown sugar, and lemon juice in skillet. Heat to simmer, stirring until sauce is smooth. Add meatballs and simmer covered 1 hour. Can be served from a chafing dish.

SERVES 20.

**A classic appetizer loved by guests of all ages.**

## WILD MUSHROOM STRUDEL

¼   cup butter
3   tablespoons chopped shallots
2½  quarts wild mushrooms, sliced (cepes, morels, chanterelles, shiitakes, oysters, etc.)
3   tablespoons flour
⅓   cup dry sherry
⅓   cup heavy cream
    salt and pepper to taste
¼   cup chopped parsley
4   sheets phyllo dough
⅓   cup clarified butter

In a deep skillet melt butter and cook shallots over medium heat until softened without browning. Add mushrooms and cook until all juice evaporates. Dust with flour; stir to prevent lumping. Add sherry, cream, salt and pepper. Cook a little more until mixture thickens. Remove from heat, spread on a pan to cool, add parsley.

Preheat oven to 400 degrees. To assemble, place a sheet of phyllo on a clean towel or napkin, brush with clarified butter. Place another sheet on top, brush again and repeat until all sheets are stacked. With phyllo stack lengthwise, place the cooled mushroom mixture in a row along the long end near you; grasp the towel, lift the edge of the sheets over the filling and roll away from you, encasing the filling snugly in the sheets. Using the towel, lift the roll and place seam down on a parchment-lined baking sheet. Brush with butter and bake until browned and crispy. Slice into serving pieces, serve warm.

SERVES 6.

**The Golden Mushroom Restaurant
Southfield, Michigan**

## SAVORY CRAB CHEESE SPREAD

8 ounces cream cheese
⅓ cup mayonnaise
1 tablespoon powdered sugar
1 tablespoon dry white wine
½ teaspoon onion juice
½ teaspoon prepared mustard
¼ teaspoon garlic salt
¼ teaspoon salt
12 ounces crabmeat, cooked or canned
   finely chopped parsley

Preheat oven to 375 degrees. Combine all ingredients, except crabmeat and parsley, blending well. Gently fold in crabmeat. Place in a greased 1-quart ceramic baking dish. Sprinkle the top with parsley. Bake for 15 minutes. Serve hot in baking dish for spreading on toast or crackers.

SERVES 8.

## COLD PIQUANT SHRIMP

2 pounds (48 medium) shrimp, cooked, shelled,
   and deveined
1½ cups vegetable oil
½ cup red wine vinegar
¼ teaspoon seasoned salt
4 drops Tabasco sauce
1½ tablespoons capers, drained
1 large red onion, peeled and sliced very thin,
   rings separated
3 bay leaves

Stir briskly or shake in jar to blend the oil, vinegar, seasoned salt, and Tabasco. Add capers. Arrange shrimp on a bed of onion rings in a glass or ceramic dish. Top shrimp with more onion rings and pour dressing over all. Break bay leaves and slip them in among the shrimp. Cover tightly and refrigerate overnight. Baste occasionally. Remove bay leaf pieces and drain, reserving marinade. Arrange the shrimp in even layers when serving. Leftover shrimp may be stored in refrigerator in reserved marinade 1-3 days.

SERVES 12.

**A perfect addition to an appetizer buffet. Complement the shrimp with cheese, fruit, and meat dishes.**

## GREEN ONION RYE MELTS

1  cup grated sharp Cheddar cheese
1  cup grated Monterey Jack cheese
1  cup finely chopped green onions
1  cup mayonnaise
7  ounces pitted black ripe olives, finely chopped
1  cup finely chopped fresh mushrooms
1  loaf cocktail rye bread

Preheat oven to 350 degrees. Mix cheeses, onions, mayonnaise, olives, and mushrooms. Spoon 1 rounded teaspoon of cheese mixture on each slice of rye bread. Place on cookie sheet. Bake for 5 minutes, or until melted. Serve warm.

SERVES 12-16.

To add panache to this party favorite, cut each bread slice with a 3-inch metal cookie cutter into hearts or flowers before topping with cheese mixture.

## HUMMUS BI TAHINI

¼  cup tahini (sesame seed paste)
⅓  cup fresh lemon juice
⅓-½  cup warm water
1  clove garlic, chopped
¾  cup dried chickpeas, cooked and drained (or 2 cups canned chickpeas, drained and rinsed)
½  teaspoon salt
   freshly ground black pepper, to taste
   GARNISH:
   olive oil
   chopped fresh parsley
4-6  pitas (or pocket bread), cut into wedges

Put the tahini, lemon juice, water, and garlic into a blender or a food processor fitted with the metal blade. Cover and process until smooth. With the machine running, gradually add the chickpeas, salt, and pepper, processing until the mixture is the consistency of a very thick paste. The mixture will thicken more when it is refrigerated; if it seems too thick after processing, add up to one-half cup more water and process again. Taste to correct seasonings. Put the hummus into a bowl and refrigerate, covered, to chill. Before serving, drizzle with olive oil and garnish with the chopped parsley. Surround with pita wedges for dipping. To store, cover and refrigerate for up to 1 week, or freeze for up to 3 months.

SERVES 8-10.

## ARTICHOKE BAGEL BITES

1   *cup marinated artichoke hearts, well drained and chopped*
1   *cup Parmesan or Romano cheese*
1   *tablespoon paprika*
1   *cup mayonnaise*
10  *mini garlic bagels*

In medium mixing bowl, combine artichoke hearts, cheese, paprika, and mayonnaise. Refrigerate 10 minutes. Preheat oven to 350 degrees. Slice mini bagels and arrange on baking sheet. Spoon 1 tablespoon artichoke mixture on top of each mini bagel half. Bake 5-10 minutes until lightly golden.

SERVES 8-10.

## CLASSIC ITALIAN STUFFED MUSHROOMS

1   *pound large mushrooms (2-3-inch caps)*
4   *tablespoons olive oil, divided*
¼   *cup chopped onion*
½   *clove garlic, finely chopped*
⅓   *cup fine, dry bread crumbs*
4   *tablespoons freshly grated Parmesan cheese*
1   *tablespoon finely chopped fresh parsley*
½   *teaspoon salt*
⅛   *teaspoon oregano*

Preheat oven to 400 degrees. Remove stems from mushrooms and place caps open side up in casserole. Set aside. Finely chop mushroom stems. Heat 2 tablespoons of olive oil in 10-inch skillet. Add mushroom stems, chopped onion, and garlic. Cook slowly until onions and garlic are slightly browned. In a bowl, combine bread crumbs, Parmesan cheese, parsley, salt, and oregano. Mix in onion, garlic and mushroom stems. Spoon mixture lightly into inverted caps. Pour remaining 2 tablespoons of olive oil into casserole. Bake for 15-20 minutes, or until mushrooms are tender and tops are browned.

SERVES 4-6.

## ZAKOPANE

6 pounds Polish kielbasa
1 cup chili sauce
¼ cup Dijon mustard
¼-½ cup vodka
¼ cup prepared horseradish
1 tablespoon dried dill
1 teaspoon caraway seed

 Wash and dry kielbasa. Cut into one-half-inch pieces. Spread on a jelly roll pan and place in a 325 degree oven for about one-half hour or until most of the fat has melted. Drain and pat dry with paper towels. Place in a baking dish and add the chili sauce, mustard, vodka, horseradish, dill, and caraway seed. Mix and refrigerate at least 8 hours, stirring occasionally. Serve thoroughly heated from a chafing dish with toothpicks on the side. Zakopane can be made ahead and frozen.

SERVES 25.

An easy, do-ahead chafing dish hors d'oeuvre.

## STUFFED MICHIGAN MORELS

25 large morels
½ cup butter
1 cup chopped onion
1 cup chopped celery
1 teaspoon salt
½ teaspoon black pepper
½ teaspoon paprika
5 cups dry bread crumbs
1½ cups coarsely chopped pecans
beaten eggs
½-1 cup melted butter

 Select large (preferably white) morels. Rinse thoroughly, trim off stems, set morels aside and chop stems. Heat butter in large, heavy skillet and sauté onion, celery, and chopped mushroom stems until tender and transparent. Stir in seasonings, bread crumbs, and pecans. Stir in enough beaten eggs to moisten mixture. Spoon filling in pastry bag fitted with a serrated metal tip and stuff morels. Set stuffed morels, points up, on a buttered baking sheet. Drizzle with melted butter and bake at 350 degrees for 20-30 minutes. Serve upright on chopped parsley or other greens.

SERVES 10-12.

The Merchant of Vino
Birmingham, Michigan

Michiganians are fortunate to have access to three native varieties of fresh morels in early May each year.

## THREE-CHEESE TORTA WITH PINE NUTS

12  ounces mascarpone (Italian cream cheese)
12  ounces goat cheese
    freshly ground pepper to taste
6   ounces Brie cheese
1   cup pine nuts
1   teaspoon olive oil

Mix the mascarpone with the goat cheese, add freshly ground pepper. Brush a small (3-cup) loaf pan with one-half teaspoon oil. Line the pan with plastic wrap, leaving a 1-inch overhang all around. Brush plastic wrap with remaining oil. Using the back of a spoon, spread one-half the mixture of mascarpone and goat cheese, then add the layer of Brie and one-half the pine nuts. Top with the remaining mascarpone and goat cheese mixture. Refrigerate for 12 hours. One hour before unmolding, remove the torta from the refrigerator. To unmold, invert the pan onto a serving platter and tap the bottom. Gently pull out loaf using the end of the plastic wrap. Evenly spread the rest of the pine nuts over the sides of the loaf. Serve chilled with crackers, slices of French bread, and fresh fruit.

SERVES 12.

**The Merchant of Vino
Birmingham, Michigan**

**A creative appetizer designed by Juliette Jonna, of the Merchant of Vino gourmet food shops.**

## MUSHROOM LOGS

½   pound fresh mushrooms, chopped
4   tablespoons butter or margarine
2   tablespoons fresh chopped chives
1   tablespoon fresh lemon juice
5   ounces light cream
2   tablespoons flour
½   teaspoon salt
14  slices white sandwich bread, crusts trimmed, rolled flat
    melted butter or margarine for brushing

Preheat oven to 400 degrees. Sauté mushrooms in the butter. Add chives, lemon juice, cream, flour, and salt. Simmer until mixture thickens, stirring constantly. Spread mixture on the bread. Roll each slice of bread around mixture. Brush with melted butter or margarine. Freeze until ready to bake. Slice each roll into 4 pieces. Bake for approximately 15 minutes or until bread is golden.

SERVES 12-14.

## NINA'S CHÈVRE PIZZA

**CRUST:**

2     *tablespoons dry yeast*
1½   *cups warm water (approximately 110 degrees)*
     *pinch of iodized sea salt*
1     *teaspoon honey*
1     *tablespoon virgin olive oil*
3     *cups unbleached flour*
½    *cup semolina flour*
     *corn meal for dusting*

To prepare crust, combine yeast, water, salt, honey, and oil in a large bowl. Add unbleached flour and semolina, stirring to make a firm dough. Knead 5 minutes. Place dough in a lightly oiled bowl and cover with a towel. Let dough rise until it has doubled in size, 1 hour. Punch dough down and transfer to a surface lightly dusted with corn meal. Cut dough into 3 equal pieces. Lightly oil 3 round 12-inch pizza pans. Roll dough slightly larger than the pan. Arrange dough on pans and pinch to make an even edge. Preheat oven to 350 degrees. Bake crusts 10 minutes, remove from oven.

**TOPPING:**

3     *logs (6 ounces each) chèvre (goat cheese), crumbled*
     *enough fresh basil leaves to cover 3 pizzas*
3     *cups seeded, chopped tomatoes, drained for 1 hour*
2     *large bell peppers, cut in thin strips*
6     *tablespoons thinly sliced black olives*
9     *tablespoons tomato purée*
1     *tablespoon fresh oregano (or 3 teaspoons dried)*
     *fresh ground pepper*
3-4   *tablespoons grated Parmesan cheese*

To assemble pizzas: Cover each crust with 6 ounces of cheese and basil leaves. Spread chopped tomatoes over leaves; arrange pepper strips and olives over tomatoes. With a spatula, spread 3 tablespoons of tomato purée over top of each pizza. Sprinkle with oregano, ground pepper, and Parmesan cheese. Bake 20-30 minutes.

MAKES 3 PIZZAS, SERVES 4 EACH.

## CRAB CUP PUFFS

½ pound crabmeat
2 tablespoons fresh lemon juice
½ clove garlic, crushed
1 tablespoon finely chopped scallions
  or green onions
1 teaspoon Worcestershire sauce
½ teaspoon dried tarragon
⅛ teaspoon ground black pepper
⅛ teaspoon cayenne pepper
1 tablespoon finely chopped fresh parsley
1 egg
1 cup mayonnaise
¼ pound butter
12 slices white sandwich bread
  paprika

(If crabmeat is frozen, defrost and press out water.) Crumble crabmeat to a uniform fineness. In a 2-quart bowl, blend lemon juice, garlic, scallions, Worcestershire sauce, tarragon, pepper, cayenne, parsley, egg, and mayonnaise. Add crabmeat. Preheat oven to 400 degrees. Melt butter in a medium sized frying pan. Trim crusts off 12 slices of bread. Flatten slightly with a rolling pin. Cut each slice into quarters. Dip each square into melted butter and push butter side down into mini muffin pans. Fill with a heaping teaspoon of crab mixture and sprinkle with paprika. Bake for 10-15 minutes until puffed and golden brown. Serve hot.

SERVES 12-16.

## SMOKED SALMON BALL

16 ounces canned salmon
8 ounces cream cheese, softened
2 teaspoons grated onion
1 teaspoon grated horseradish
1 teaspoon fresh lemon juice
¼ teaspoon salt
¼ teaspoon liquid smoke
¼ cup finely chopped pecans
2 tablespoons finely chopped parsley

Drain and flake salmon, removing skin and bones. Combine salmon, cream cheese, onion, horseradish, lemon juice, salt, and liquid smoke. Mix thoroughly. Chill several hours. Combine pecans and parsley. Shape salmon mixture into a ball or log and roll in nut mixture. Chill again. Serve with assorted crackers.

SERVES 12.

Can be made ahead and frozen. A perfect appetizer for entertaining all year round.

## CHANCHA EN PIEDRA

2 pounds fresh, ripe tomatoes, peeled
1 fresh hot pepper (jalapeño or chili), diced
   (or ½-¾ teaspoon ground cayenne pepper)
1 clove garlic, peeled
1 tablespoon olive oil
   pinch of cayenne pepper
   salt to taste
1 crusty loaf of French bread, unsliced

Purée tomatoes, fresh hot pepper, and garlic in a blender. Add oil, cayenne, and salt and mix well. (An alternate, traditional method would be to grind together the garlic, salt, and cayenne using a large mortar and pestle. Add diced pepper and pulverize, then add tomatoes and mash until soupy. Stir in oil, mix well.) Refrigerate at least 1 hour (or overnight). Serve in a large mortar or bowl with a loaf of bread. To eat, break off small chunks of bread and dip into tomato mixture.

SERVES 4.

**A regional dish of Talca, Chile, where it's known as the poor man's summertime tea. It is especially good when served with a crisp white wine.**

## OYSTERS ROCKEFELLER

36 fresh oysters, opened on a half shell
 1 cup oyster water, reserved from draining
   oysters
 1 cup water
¼ cup shallots
 1 small sprig fresh thyme
½ cup trimmed, packed, fresh spinach leaves
 2 small celery ribs
 1 cup unsalted butter
 1 ounce Pernod liqueur
 1 tablespoon Worcestershire sauce
½ cup ground, toasted bread crumbs

Mix oyster water and water and boil 5 minutes. Grind all vegetables in chopper or food processor. Add chopped vegetables and cook 20 minutes until thickened. Stir in butter; when melted remove from heat. Add Pernod and Worcestershire sauce. Spoon sauce over oysters. Sprinkle each with bread crumbs. Set in a hot oven (475 degrees) for 5 minutes. Serve hot.

SERVES 6.

**This recipe is based on the all-American classic first served in the 1870s in New Orleans.**

## CHICKEN LIVER ALMOND PÂTÉ

½ cup unsalted butter
1 small onion, chopped fine
8 ounces chicken livers, washed and deveined
1 rounded teaspoon mild French mustard
1 level teaspoon ground nutmeg
  salt and black pepper
2 tablespoons brandy
  juice of ½ orange
2 tablespoons heavy cream
¼ cup chopped blanched almonds
1 teaspoon chopped fresh or dried chives
  (optional)

Melt 2 tablespoons butter in a frying pan and gently cook the onion until soft. Add the chicken livers and cook gently, stirring once or twice for five minutes. Add the mustard, nutmeg, 4 tablespoons butter, salt, and pepper. When the butter has melted, remove from heat and add brandy, orange juice, and cream. Purée in a blender until smooth, or press through a sieve. Stir the chopped almonds and all but a sprinkling of the chives into the mixture. Transfer to a medium-size soufflé dish and sprinkle top with the remaining chives. Melt the remaining 2 tablespoons butter in a pan for a minute. Remove from heat and allow to stand for 2 minutes. Pour melted butter through a fine sieve over the top of the pâté. Allow to cool. Cover with foil and chill well before serving.

SERVES 6-8.

An elegant first course. Serve with cornichons, thin toast points, and a crisp, dry champagne.

## SWEET RED PEPPER DIP

5 large sweet red peppers
4 large ripe tomatoes
5 cloves garlic, peeled
3½ ounces ground almonds
½ cup mayonnaise
1 tablespoon red wine vinegar
¼-½ cup olive oil
½ teaspoon salt
¼ teaspoon freshly ground pepper
2½ teaspoons cayenne pepper

Broil peppers until skins are blistered and blackened all over. Cool, then peel and seed. Peel and seed tomatoes. Chop pulp coarsely, and blot on paper towels. Place peppers, tomatoes, garlic, almonds, mayonnaise, and red wine vinegar in food processor or blender. Purée, slowly adding olive oil until mixture is consistency of thick sauce. Season with salt and pepper. Stir in cayenne. Chill for at least 3 hours to blend flavors.

SERVES 8-10.

A striking appetizer when served with green pepper strips, yellow zucchini slices, mozzarella cheese chunks, and crunchy bread.

The aspen leaves must all be cold

They shiver in a gentle breeze

While black-eyed Susans shine like gold

And lilies buzz with fuzzy bees.

# BREADS

## AMELANCHIER MUFFINS

½  cup butter
1 ¼  cups sugar
2  eggs
2  cups flour
½  teaspoon salt
2  teaspoons baking powder
½  cup milk
2  cups Juneberries (or 2 cups blueberries or 1 cup dried Michigan cherries, snipped)
2  tablespoons superfine sugar

Preheat oven to 375 degrees. In a large bowl, cream the butter and sugar. Beat in the eggs one at a time. Sift together flour, salt, and baking powder. Add alternately with milk to creamed mixture. Fold in fruit. Grease muffin pans well, dust lightly with flour. Fill each cup three-quarters full with batter. Sprinkle with superfine sugar. Bake 30 minutes or until done. Allow muffins to cool 5 minutes before removing from pan.

MAKES 24 MEDIUM MUFFINS.

The Amelanchier tree, commonly known as Juneberry, has small edible berries. When Juneberries are out of season, fresh blueberries or dried Michigan cherries are tasty substitutes.

## MINI SPOONFRUIT MUFFINS

1  cup whole wheat flour
1  cup flour
4  tablespoons sugar or honey
1  tablespoon baking powder
   pinch of salt
¼  teaspoon ground allspice
2  whole large eggs (or 3 egg whites)
1  cup milk or buttermilk
4  tablespoons vegetable oil
   about ½ cup spoonfruit or marmalade

Preheat oven to 375 degrees. Grease well and flour well 2 mini-muffin pans; set aside. In a medium-size mixing bowl, blend together flour, sugar, baking powder, salt and allspice. Mix eggs, milk, and oil together in another mixing bowl. Gradually stir liquid ingredients into flour mixture until moistened. Spoon 1 rounded teaspoon of batter into each muffin cup, add about 1 teaspoon of spoonfruit, then additional batter to cover the fruit. Bake about 12-15 minutes or until golden brown.

MAKES 24 MINI MUFFINS.

An ideal muffin for a breakfast meeting. Try several different spoonfruit or jam flavors for variety.

## BLUEBERRY CORN MUFFINS

1   cup flour
1   cup corn meal
4   tablespoons sugar
3   teaspoons baking powder
    pinch of salt
2   whole large eggs (or 3 egg whites)
1   cup milk
4   tablespoons vegetable oil
¼   teaspoon ground cinnamon
1   cup blueberries

Preheat oven to 375 degrees. In a medium mixing bowl, blend together flour, corn meal, sugar, baking powder, and salt. Make a well in the center and add the eggs, milk, oil, and cinnamon. Mix liquid ingredients together, slowly stirring in the dry ingredients. When well blended add blueberries. Grease and flour muffin pan or use paper liners. Spoon batter into pan, filling each cup two-thirds full. Bake for 20-30 minutes until golden brown.

MAKES 7-8 MEDIUM MUFFINS.

**A hint of cinnamon in this recipe enhances as well as entices the palate.**

## APPLESAUCE DATE MUFFINS

2   cups sifted flour
3   tablespoons sugar
4   teaspoons baking powder
½   teaspoon salt
2   eggs, beaten
1   cup milk
½   cup applesauce
3   tablespoons melted butter
½   cup chopped dates

Preheat oven to 400 degrees. Sift flour, sugar, baking powder, and salt together. Combine eggs and milk and add to dry ingredients, stirring only until moistened. Add applesauce and butter and blend well. Fold in chopped dates. Fill well-greased muffin pans two-thirds full and bake for 20 minutes.

MAKES 12 MUFFINS.

## APPLE BREAD

1  cup sugar
½  cup margarine or butter
2  eggs
2  tablespoons sour milk or buttermilk
1  teaspoon vanilla
2  cups flour
½  teaspoon salt
1  teaspoon baking soda
2  cups peeled and cubed apples
   TOPPING:
2  tablespoons margarine or butter
2  tablespoons flour
2  tablespoons brown sugar
1  teaspoon cinnamon

Preheat oven to 350 degrees. Cream sugar and margarine. Add unbeaten eggs, sour milk, and vanilla. Beat until well mixed and smooth. Mix together flour, salt, and baking soda. Continue to beat egg mixture while gradually adding dry ingredients. Fold in diced apples. Pour into 4½ x 8½ x 2½-inch loaf pan. To prepare topping, melt margarine. Add flour, brown sugar, and cinnamon. Mix and then crumble and sprinkle on top of unbaked loaf. Bake for 1 hour.

MAKES 1 LOAF.

## SPICED ZUCCHINI BREAD

3  eggs
1  cup vegetable oil
2  cups sugar
2  cups grated zucchini
3  cups sifted flour
1  teaspoon salt
1  teaspoon baking soda
¼  teaspoon baking powder
3  tablespoons cinnamon
1  cup chopped pecans
1  cup raisins

Preheat oven to 350 degrees. In a large mixing bowl, blend eggs, oil, and sugar. Combine flour, salt, baking soda, baking powder, and cinnamon in a separate bowl. Add grated zucchini alternately with the dry ingredients to the egg mixture. Add pecans and raisins and mix. Pour into 2 greased 8½ x 4½ x 3-inch loaf pans. Bake for 50-60 minutes until cake tester comes out clean.

MAKES 2 LOAVES.

## LEMON NUT BREAD

grated zest and juice of 2 lemons
1½ cups sugar
1 cup vegetable oil
6 eggs
1⅔ cups flour, divided
2 teaspoons baking powder
pinch of salt
1 cup chopped walnuts
2 teaspoons superfine sugar

Preheat oven to 300 degrees. In a large mixing bowl, combine grated lemon zest, lemon juice, sugar, and oil. Mix well; add eggs one at a time, beating well after each addition. Add 1⅓ cups of flour, baking powder, and salt. Toss walnuts in reserved one-third cup flour and add to batter. Pour into 2 greased loaf pans (about 5½ x 3½ x 2 ½ inches). Sprinkle with superfine sugar. Bake 1 hour. Cool on a rack for 10 minutes before removing from pans.

MAKES 2 SMALL LOAVES.

**This rich tea bread is neither too sweet nor too tart. Slice thin and serve with a pot of your favorite hot brew.**

## BLUEBERRY COFFEE SQUARE

2 cups flour
2 teaspoons baking powder
½ teaspoon salt
¼ cup butter or margarine
¾ cup light brown sugar
1 egg
½ cup milk
2 cups blueberries
TOPPING:
½ cup brown sugar
⅓ cup flour
½ teaspoon cinnamon
¼ cup butter or margarine

Preheat oven to 350 degrees. Thoroughly mix together flour, baking powder, and salt and set aside. In a mixer bowl, cream butter and sugar, add egg. Gradually add flour mixture and milk alternately until dry ingredients are moistened. Fold in berries. Pour into a well-greased 9-inch square pan. Blend together topping ingredients and sprinkle on batter. Bake for 45-50 minutes. Place pan on rack to cool.

SERVES 8-10.

## WALNUT RAISIN ROUND

¾  cup milk
¼  ounce (1 scant tablespoon) dry yeast
2  teaspoons granulated sugar
3  teaspoons light brown sugar
¾  teaspoon salt
2  eggs
½  cup butter, softened
3  cups whole wheat flour
½  cup chopped walnuts
¼  cup dark raisins
¼  cup light raisins
1  egg white

Scald milk, remove from heat. Allow to cool to lukewarm. In a large electric mixer bowl, add milk and sugars. Sprinkle yeast over surface and allow to proof 10-12 minutes. On slow speed gradually add salt, eggs, and butter. Slowly add flour until batter thickens and shreds from beaters. Fold in walnuts and raisins. Gather dough, set into a greased bowl. Cover and set in a warm place to rise. When dough has doubled, punch down and knead lightly for 1 minute. Set into a buttered 1½-2 quart soufflé dish or casserole. Allow dough to double again. Preheat oven to 375 degrees. Brush dough lightly with beaten egg white and bake 30-40 minutes. Cool in soufflé dish or casserole on a rack before removing.

Makes 1 loaf.

**You can't beat the combin-ation of walnuts and raisins in a slice of warm bread with butter.**

## POTTER'S BROWN BREAD

¾  cup brown sugar
1  teaspoon salt
½  teaspoon baking soda
2  cups whole wheat flour
1  cup unbleached flour
1½ cups buttermilk
½  cup molasses
1  egg
½  cup raisins

Preheat oven to 325 degrees. Mix all ingredients well in a large bowl. Generously grease a 1 quart or 8½ x 5 x 3-inch loaf pan (preferably glass or ceramic). Spoon in batter. Bake for about 1 hour or until a toothpick or skewer inserted in center comes out clean. Allow to cool in pan, 10-15 minutes. Invert on a baking rack and cool completely. Freezes well.

Makes 1 loaf.

**An unsteamed version of a traditional favorite. Measure ingredients precisely for maximum flavor.**

## ENGLISH TEA LOAF

1 cup flour
2 cups whole wheat flour
1 cup granulated sugar
1 teaspoon salt
2 cups sour milk (or 2 cups milk mixed
  with 2 tablespoons of vinegar—let stand
  for 15 minutes)
2 teaspoons baking soda
1 cup chopped walnuts
1 cup raisins

Preheat oven to 350 degrees. In a large mixing bowl combine flours, sugar, and salt. In a 1-quart pitcher or bowl, stir baking soda into sour milk with very quick strokes and immediately pour into flour mixture. (Milk will bubble and foam as soda is added.) Stir until mixed. Quickly fold in nuts and raisins. Pour into 2 lightly greased 8½ x 4½ x 2½-inch bread tins. Bake for about 50 minutes. To make muffins instead of loaves, use lightly greased or paper lined muffin tins. Bake for about 15-20 minutes. The texture of the tea bread improves for slicing after 24 hours.

MAKES 2 LOAVES OR 24 MUFFINS.

**For tea-time sandwiches, fill thinly sliced bread with cream cheese or fruit butter.**

## TEA SCONES

4 cups flour
4 tablespoons sugar
2 tablespoons baking powder
½ cup unsalted butter, chilled, diced
1 cup currants
4 eggs, lightly beaten
⅔ cup cream or milk
1 egg white, lightly beaten
  coarse sugar

Preheat oven to 425 degrees. Sift together flour, sugar, and baking powder into a bowl. Add the butter and blend into dry ingredients with fork, reducing until texture is coarse, resembling pebbles. Stir in currants. In separate bowl, combine eggs and cream, mix well. Stir liquid into dry ingredients and mix until all flour is incorporated. Shape into ball. Turn out onto a floured board and roll to a 1-inch-thick circle. Cut rounds about 2½ inches in diameter using cookie cutter or a glass. Place rounds on lightly floured baking sheet. Brush tops with lightly beaten egg white. Sprinkle with coarse sugar. Bake 12-15 minutes. Remove from baking sheet and cool on a rack. Serve warm, plain or with butter or clotted cream and jam.

MAKES 2 DOZEN.

## Irish Soda Bread

4 cups flour
4 tablespoons sugar
1 teaspoon salt
1 teaspoon baking powder
1 teaspoon baking soda
¾ cup butter, room temperature
2 eggs
1 cup raisins
1 tablespoon caraway seeds
1½ cups buttermilk
1 egg white

Preheat oven to 375 degrees. In large mixing bowl, sift together flour, sugar, salt, baking powder, and baking soda. Add butter gradually to flour mixture. Add eggs, one at a time, beating well after each addition. Fold in raisins and caraway seeds. Slowly blend in buttermilk until mixture takes shape. Dust with flour if dough is sticky, and form into a ball. Set in a well-greased 9-inch glass pie pan. Flatten dough to fill pan and brush top with lightly beaten egg white. Bake for 1 hour or until toothpick comes out clean when inserted in center and edges are lightly golden. Allow to cool in pan 10 minutes, then remove and cool on rack completely before cutting.

MAKES 1 LOAF.

**Don't wait for St. Patrick's Day to try this. It's great served with winter stews of all kinds!**

## Americana Drop Biscuits

2 cups sifted flour
2½ teaspoons baking powder
2 tablespoons sugar
½ teaspoon salt
4 tablespoons butter or shortening, diced
⅔ cup milk
1 cup pared, finely chopped apple
1½ teaspoons grated orange rind
½ cup chopped raisins

Preheat oven to 450 degrees. In a medium bowl, mix together flour, baking powder, sugar, and salt. Add diced butter and reduce to smaller particles using a fork. Add milk and stir just until batter is moist. Add fruits and grated rind and stir vigorously until mixture forms a soft dough. Drop from a teaspoon onto an ungreased baking sheet. Bake for 12 minutes.

MAKES 18 BISCUITS.

**Chopped fruits added to an old-fashioned biscuit make it a perfect accompaniment at tea time.**

## VILLAGE INN CORN BREAD

1   cup corn meal
1   cup buttermilk
1   cup flour
3   tablespoons sugar
½   teaspoon baking soda
1   tablespoon baking powder
4   tablespoons corn oil
2   eggs
1   cup creamed corn
4   ounces canned jalapeño peppers, diced
    (optional)
1   cup grated Cheddar cheese
¼   cup grated Monterey Jack cheese

Preheat oven to 350 degrees. In a large bowl, mix corn meal and buttermilk and allow to set for one-half hour. Add remaining ingredients and mix. Pour into a greased 8 x 8-inch baking dish and bake for 30 minutes, until golden brown. Serve warm.

SERVES 8-10.

**A new twist on a traditional favorite, from the owner of the Village Inn in Mendocino, California.**

## COUNTRY BEER BREAD

3    cups self-rising flour
1½   teaspoons sugar
¼    teaspoon salt
12   ounces beer

Preheat oven to 350 degrees. In a large mixing bowl, thoroughly mix together flour, sugar, salt, and beer. Pour into a greased bread pan (about 9 x 5 x 3 inches). Bake for 45 minutes. Serve warm.

MAKES 1 LOAF.

**Makes a crusty bread for family meals. An excellent accompaniment to hearty soups and stews.**

## CALZONE—"PIZZA IN A POCKET"

CRUST:

1   *cup hot water (108-110 degrees)*
¼   *ounce (1 scant tablespoon) dry yeast*
3   *cups unbleached flour*
1   *teaspoon salt*
2   *tablespoons olive oil*

 Combine flour and salt in an electric mixer bowl. Dissolve yeast in one-half cup hot water, stir well. Gradually add yeast mixture to flour mixing well. Mix olive oil with remaining one-half cup of water and, with machine running, beat into dough. Knead dough on a lightly floured surface or use dough hook of electric mixer. Knead about 7-8 minutes by hand, 5 minutes with dough hook, or until dough is smooth and elastic. Transfer dough to a lightly oiled 3-quart bowl, cover and set in a warm place to rise (about 1 hour). When dough has doubled, punch down, set on lightly floured surface, flatten and divide into 4 equal parts. Cover and let rest a few minutes.

FILLING:

½   *cup tomato sauce*
12  *thin slices prosciutto (Italian smoked ham), shredded*
2   *cups mozzarella cheese*
4   *tablespoons Parmesan cheese*
¼   *cup pine nuts*
    *freshly ground black pepper*
    *olive oil for brushing dough*

To assemble calzones: Preheat oven to 450 degrees. Roll or shape pieces of dough into approximately 6-inch circles. Using a knife, score a line down the center of each circle. Dividing the filling ingredients into 4 equal portions, spoon sauce, then prosciutto, cheeses, and pine nuts onto one side of each round of dough. Season with pepper. Fold the other side of the dough over the filling and pinch around edges to seal. Transfer calzones to a heavy cookie sheet lightly dusted with corn meal. Vent tops with a few holes. Brush lightly with olive oil and bake 15-20 minutes until golden brown.

SERVES 4.

Calzone dough can be used as a basic pizza dough.

## SCUPPY'S CRESCENT ROLLS

1   cup milk
½   cup butter
½   cup sugar
1   teaspoon salt
3   large eggs
½   ounce (2 scant tablespoons) dry yeast
¼   cup warm water
4½-5   cups bread flour

 In a small saucepan, scald milk, remove from heat. Add butter, sugar, and salt. Allow to cool to room temperature. In a large electric mixer bowl, beat eggs, add milk-butter mixture. Dissolve yeast in one-quarter cup water (105-115 degrees). Add yeast to bowl. With mixer running, gradually add 2 cups flour. Keep adding flour in the same manner until dough is firm. Knead dough either by hand (200 times) or with a dough hook in mixer for 10 minutes or until smooth. Put dough in a lightly greased bowl. Cover and set in a warm place to rise (1-1½ hours). When dough has doubled, punch down with fist. Knead 10 minutes. Repeat rising and kneading process again. Cut dough into 5 equal parts. Roll each one into a 10-inch diameter circle. Cut each circle into 8 wedges. Roll each wedge from base to point and bend both ends to form a crescent. Set on a buttered cookie sheet to rest dough. Preheat oven to 375 degrees and bake for 10-15 minutes.

MAKES 40 ROLLS.

If a yield of 40 rolls is overwhelming, double wrap and keep extras in the freezer up to 3 months.

## DILLY CHEESE BREAD

¼   ounce (1 scant tablespoon) dry yeast
¼   cup warm water (110-115 degrees)
1   cup cottage cheese, room temperature
2   tablespoons sugar
4   tablespoons butter, diced
1   egg, lightly beaten
¼   cup minced onion
2½   cups all-purpose flour
2   teaspoons dill weed
1   teaspoon salt
¼   teaspoon baking soda
    butter and coarse salt for top

Dissolve yeast in water for 5 minutes. In a large bowl, combine cheese, sugar, and butter and stir until blended. Add egg and onion, stir in yeast. Combine flour, dill, salt, and baking soda. Gradually beat into yeast-cheese mixture until dough is firm. Turn dough into a lightly greased bowl, cover and set in a warm place (85 degrees) to rise for 1 hour. Punch dough down with fist and turn into a buttered 2-quart soufflé dish. Cover again and allow to rise 1 hour. Bake in a preheated 350 degree oven for 40-50 minutes until golden. Brush with butter and coarse salt.

MAKES 1 ROUND LOAF.

## NANA'S COFFEE CAKE ROLL

½  ounce (2 scant tablespoons) dry yeast
½  cup warm water
3  cups sugar, divided
12  cups flour
6  eggs, beaten
1  cup sour cream
1½  cups butter, divided
2  cups buttermilk
1  tablespoon salt
2  cups yellow raisins
2  teaspoons cinnamon

 In a small cup or bowl, dissolve yeast in water with one teaspoon of the sugar. In a large bowl, combine flour and two cups of the remaining sugar. Add beaten eggs and sour cream, mixing well. In a saucepan, heat one cup of the butter, buttermilk, and salt until butter melts. Slowly pour into batter, adding yeast mixture. Mix well. Knead in bowl or on a lightly floured board 1-2 minutes. Place in a large greased bowl, turn dough over once, cover and set to rise in a warm place until doubled in size (about 2 hours).

Punch down and divide dough into 4 equal portions. On a lightly floured surface, roll out each portion to form a 12-inch square. Melt the remaining half cup of butter. Brush all 4 squares with a total of one-third of the butter, reserving the rest for the topping. Sprinkle each square with raisins. Mix remaining sugar with cinnamon and sprinkle three-quarters of the mixture on the squares. Roll them up jelly-roll fashion. Set on well greased baking sheets. Cover and allow to rise until doubled (about 1 hour). Preheat oven to 325 degrees. Brush tops with remaining butter, sprinkle with sugar-cinnamon mixture. Bake 50-60 minutes. Cool thoroughly before slicing.

MAKES 4 LOAVES.

## BARKAS (CZECH) SWEET BREAD

1  cake yeast
¼  cup lukewarm milk
1  teaspoon sugar
8  tablespoons butter or margarine
2  tablespoons oil
1¾  cups hot milk
¾  cup sugar
1  teaspoon salt
1  large egg
6  cups flour

 Dissolve yeast in one-quarter cup of lukewarm milk and teaspoon of sugar. (If using rapid or dry package yeast, follow directions on packet.) Place butter or margarine and oil in a large bowl, add milk. When dissolved, add sugar, salt, and beaten egg and stir. Add yeast and flour. Mix well. Set in warm place to rise. When doubled in size, remove from pan, divide in half. Divide each half into 3 equal parts. Roll each part into a strip, using your hands, not a roller. In a well-greased 12 x 18-inch jelly roll pan, secure 3 strips at the top and start to braid, twisting each strip. Repeat with the other three strips. Cover and let rise again. When doubled in size, bake in preheated 350 degree oven on middle rack 30 minutes or until a toothpick comes out clean.

MAKES 2 LOAVES.

This braided Czechoslovakian bread makes an attractive brunch treat.

Don't get near the stove—it's hot

So's the toaster, so's the pot.

# Soups

## TOMATO-FENNEL SOUP

4 tablespoons unsalted butter
½ cup thinly sliced leeks, white part only
¼ cup thinly sliced shallots
1 large bulb of fennel, trimmed, core removed,
   sliced into thin strips (reserve feathery greens
   for garnish)
3 cups canned plum tomatoes with juice
5 whole fresh basil leaves
   salt and freshly ground black pepper
   GARNISH:
   garlic croutons
   freshly grated Parmesan cheese

In a large saucepan, melt the butter and sauté the leeks and shallots until softened, about 5 minutes. Add fennel and sauté until fennel begins to soften, about 8-10 minutes. Add tomatoes, crushing them a bit with a wooden spoon. Stir in the basil leaves and simmer for 20-25 minutes until fennel is completely soft. Remove basil leaves and purée soup in small batches in a food processor until smooth. Season to taste with salt and pepper. Serve garnished with croutons, chopped fennel greens, and Parmesan cheese.

SERVES 4.

**Martha Stewart**
**Food and Entertainment Author**

**Martha Stewart appeared at a Cranbrook Auxiliary fund-raising event and, as an added bonus, contributed three special recipes to *Cranbrook Reflections*. See also Vegetables, Pasta, and Rice.**

## CRANBROOK GARDEN GAZPACHO

1 small cucumber, peeled
3 ripe tomatoes
½ green pepper
½ small onion
1 clove garlic
½ cup tomato juice
2 tablespoons olive oil
2 tablespoons red wine vinegar
1 teaspoon salt
¼ teaspoon pepper
   GARNISH:
½ cup sour cream
1 green pepper, diced
1 tomato, seeded and diced
3 celery stalks, trimmed and diced
1 cup croutons

Cut up vegetables and put into a blender along with tomato juice; purée for 5 seconds. Add olive oil, vinegar, salt, and pepper. Blend 1 minute. Chill thoroughly for 2-4 hours. Serve cold. Garnish each bowl with a dollop of sour cream and a sprinkle of diced vegetables and croutons.

SERVES 6.

**A simple version of everyone's favorite summer soup.**

## GARDEN VICHYSSOISE

2   tablespoons oil
1   cup unpeeled, thinly sliced potato
1   cup chopped green onions
1   large cucumber, peeled and diced
2   cups shredded lettuce
¾   teaspoon finely chopped fresh dill (leaves only)
3½  cups chicken broth (homemade or canned)
1   teaspoon salt
    freshly ground black pepper
1   cup sour cream

Heat oil in a 4-quart soup pot. Add potato and onion and cook over medium heat 5 minutes until onion is softened. Add cucumber, lettuce, dill, broth, salt and dash of pepper. Bring to a boil, reduce heat and cover. Simmer 15 minutes, stirring occasionally, until vegetables are very tender. Remove from heat, allow to cool. Add sour cream. Purée the mixture in batches in a blender until smooth. Soup may be served hot or cold.

SERVES 6.

**A variation of the original potato and leek soup created by Chef Louis Diat in 1910.**

## CUCUMBER SOUP EMMELINE

4   cups peeled and coarsely chopped cucumbers
2   cups chicken broth
2   cups light cream or half & half
½   cup chopped chives
½   cup chopped celery leaves
6   sprigs of parsley
6   tablespoons soft butter or margarine
4   tablespoons flour
    salt and pepper to taste
GARNISH:
cucumber slices, unpeeled
lemon rind curls

In a bowl combine all ingredients. Process mixture by batches in blender on medium speed until smooth. Season with salt and pepper to taste. Garnish with cucumber slices and lemon rind curls.

SERVES 4.

**A refreshing summer soup which requires "no cooking."**

## ROSEMARY AUTUMN BISQUE

1   pound butternut squash, peeled, seeded,
    and diced
2   green apples, peeled and cored
1   medium onion, chopped
4   cups chicken stock
2   slices white bread, trimmed and cubed
1   teaspoon fresh rosemary (or ½ teaspoon dried)
1   teaspoon fresh marjoram (or ½ teaspoon dried)
    salt and freshly ground pepper to taste
2   egg yolks
¼   cup light cream or milk
    GARNISH:
    Italian parsley or cilantro leaves

In a heavy 3-quart saucepan combine squash, apples, onion, stock, bread, and seasonings. Bring to a boil and simmer uncovered until squash is tender (40-50 minutes). Purée soup in batches in a blender until smooth; return to pan. In a small bowl, beat together egg yolks and cream or milk. Whisk 2 tablespoons of hot soup into the yolk and cream mixture. Slowly pour this mixture back into the soup base, whisking constantly. Reheat gently; be careful not to boil. Serve hot. Decorate each bowl with parsley leaves. Soup can be frozen in advance, just prior to adding yolks and cream. At serving time defrost, heat, then add yolks and cream following the instructions above.

SERVES 6.

## PEANUT BUTTER-PUMPKIN SOUP

4   tablespoons unsalted butter
4   cups pumpkin pie filling
2   cups puréed sweet potatoes
1   cup peanut butter
6   cups chicken or turkey broth
1   teaspoon freshly ground black pepper
1   teaspoon salt
    GARNISH:
    chopped chives
    sour cream

Melt butter in a soup pot over medium heat. Stir in pie filling, sweet potatoes and peanut butter. Add broth, pepper and salt; stir well until smooth. Reduce heat and simmer for 20 minutes. To serve, garnish soup with chives and sour cream.

SERVES 8.

**A velvety and intensely flavored soup. Just a cupful will satisfy any appetite.**

## CARROT-RICE SOUP WITH MANGO CHUTNEY

2   tablespoons butter or margarine
1   large onion, chopped
3   cups thinly sliced carrots
1   cup sliced celery
3   tablespoons rice
½   cup dry white wine
4   cups chicken broth
½   cup bottled mango chutney
4   tablespoons heavy cream
    salt and pepper to taste

 Heat butter in a large saucepan. Add onion and cook over moderately low heat until softened. Add carrots, celery, and rice and cook for 1 minute. Add wine and cook an additional minute. Add chicken broth, bring to a boil and simmer for 20 minutes or until the rice and carrots are tender. Stir in chutney. Purée soup in batches in a blender or food processor; return to pan. Stir in cream, salt and pepper to taste (additional broth may be added to thin the soup if desired). Heat and serve.

SERVES 4.

## SUNCHOKE-LEEK SOUP WITH GOUDA CHEESE

2   tablespoons unsalted butter
1   small onion, finely chopped
3   leeks, white part only, finely chopped
3   cups chicken stock
1   large carrot, peeled and grated
3   sunchokes (Jerusalem artichokes) (7 ounces),
    peeled and grated
6   medium potatoes (preferably yellow), peeled
    and cut into large chunks
    salt and freshly ground black pepper
2   cups milk
1   cup grated Gouda cheese
    GARNISH:
2   tablespoons minced chives

 In a large pot, melt the butter over medium heat. Add onion and leeks and cook about 10 minutes or until softened, stirring frequently. Add chicken stock, carrot, and sunchokes; stir and bring to a simmer. Add potatoes, do not stir; cover and cook until the potatoes are very tender, about 25 minutes. Remove the cooked potatoes with a slotted spoon and push through a coarse sieve. Return sieved potatoes to soup, stir, and season to taste with salt and pepper. Bring soup to a boil over medium-high heat. Stir in milk; when soup returns to a simmer, add cheese. Be careful not to boil again. Adjust seasoning. Serve hot garnished with chives.

SERVES 6.

## Mussel, Spinach, and Brie Soup

**Mussels:**

18   mussels
½   cup dry white wine
    few parsley stems
15   crushed peppercorns
1   sprig thyme
1   clove garlic, crushed
4   shallots, chopped
½   cup chopped mushrooms

 Check mussels and discard any open ones. Soak in cold salt water for 1 hour, drain and rinse with fresh water. In a stainless steel saucepan bring everything except mussels to a boil. Add mussels, cover tightly, and over high heat, steam until shells open. Remove from heat, strain juice through cloth and reserve. Cool mussels, remove from shells, remove beards and cut mussels into halves.

**Soup:**

⅓   cup unsalted butter
⅓   cup sliced leeks
⅓   cup diced onion
¼   cup flour
3   cups clam broth
    mussel juice
1   cup packed spinach leaves
½   cup ripe Brie cheese, rind removed
½   cup heavy cream
**Garnish:**
    croutons

In a heavy saucepan melt the butter, add vegetables and sauté until transparent. Add flour, stir 1 minute. Add clam broth and reserved mussel juice, bring to a boil, simmer 15 minutes. Remove from heat, add spinach, Brie, and cream and stir until smooth. Taste and correct seasoning. Before serving, reheat without boiling. Add mussels and serve. May be garnished with croutons.

SERVES 6.

**The Golden Mushroom Restaurant
Southfield, Michigan**

## AUNT JEAN'S POLISH MUSHROOM SOUP

4   ounces large dried mushrooms
2   quarts chicken or beef stock
2   cups sour cream
1   rounded tablespoon flour
    salt and pepper to taste
1   pound egg noodles, freshly cooked

Rinse sand off mushrooms and soak overnight in enough water to cover. Bring stock to a boil. Swish mushrooms in water to shake out remaining sand; slice into one-quarter-inch strips and add to boiling stock. Strain the mushroom water through clean terry cloth to remove sand and add this liquid to soup. Cook until mushrooms are tender, one-half hour. In a large mixing bowl, beat sour cream and flour with electric mixer, gradually adding hot soup (liquid only) until bowl is full. Pour from bowl back into pan on stove, stirring constantly. Bring back to boiling point, season with salt and pepper to taste, and pour over freshly cooked noodles.

SERVES 6-8.

## CARROT-THYME SOUP

6    cups chicken stock
1½   pounds carrots, peeled and sliced 1 inch thick
1    medium onion, diced
3    tablespoons butter or margarine
½    cup heavy cream
1½   tablespoons minced fresh thyme
     (or ¾ tablespoon dried)
     salt and pepper to taste
     GARNISH:
½    cup sour cream or plain yogurt
6    tablespoons chopped chives

In a large saucepan or soup pot bring chicken stock to a boil. Add carrots and simmer for 20 minutes or until tender. Purée in a blender until smooth; set aside. Heat butter in pot. Add onion and cook over medium heat until soft. Stir in carrot purée, heavy cream, thyme, salt and pepper. Heat and serve. Garnish with a dollop of sour cream or yogurt and a sprinkling of chopped chives. To serve cold, chill several hours.

SERVES 6.

## CREAM OLGA

8 tablespoons butter
5 bunches scallions (or 30 green onions),
   finely chopped, including tops
2 tablespoons flour
1 teaspoon salt
½ teaspoon ground black pepper
5 cups chicken broth
¾ pound mushrooms, thinly sliced
1¼ cups light cream or half & half
GARNISH:
whipped cream
parsley sprigs

 In a 6-quart Dutch oven, heat butter. Add scallions and cook covered over low heat for 10 minutes (be careful not to brown). Remove from heat and stir in flour, salt, and pepper. When the mixture is smooth, slowly add the broth. Return to heat, stirring; bring to a boil and let simmer for 10 minutes uncovered. Remove from heat, add one-half pound mushrooms. In batches, purée soup in a blender. Return soup to pot, stir in half & half, reheat. When hot, add remaining mushrooms and serve at once. (Do not let mushrooms cook.) Garnish with dollops of whipped cream and parsley sprigs.

SERVES 4-6.

## SUMMER SQUASH SOUP WITH FRESH HERBS

½ pound yellow crookneck squash, cut in 1-inch-
   thick rounds
1½ pounds zucchini, cut in 1-inch-thick rounds
½ pound pattypan (cymling or scallop) squash,
   quartered
3½ cups chicken broth
1 large onion, sliced thin (1⅓ cups)
1 teaspoon minced garlic
1 teaspoon salt
¼ teaspoon pepper
2 tablespoons finely chopped fresh basil
   chopped parsley
1 tablespoon fresh lemon juice
1 cup buttermilk or plain low-fat yogurt
GARNISH:
chopped fresh basil or parsley

 Bring all squash, the broth, onion, garlic, salt and pepper to a boil in a large saucepan. Reduce heat, cover and simmer 20 to 25 minutes until vegetables are very tender. Cool slightly. In food processor or blender, process half the mixture at a time until smooth, add the basil, parsley, and lemon juice to purée and process 5 seconds. Pour into a large container or bowl; stir to mix well. Cover and chill at least 6 hours or overnight. To serve, add the buttermilk; whisk until blended. Garnish with chopped basil or parsley.

SERVES 6.

## MICHIGAN NAVY BEAN SOUP

 1 *pound dried Michigan navy beans*
 2 *quarts water (twice)*
 1 *ham bone or smoked ham hock*
 1 *large onion, finely chopped*
1 ½ *cups finely chopped celery*
 1 *whole bay leaf*
 1 *large clove garlic, crushed*
 1 *tablespoon chopped parsley*
 ½ *teaspoon salt*
 ¼ *teaspoon pepper*
 1 *teaspoon sugar*
 ¼ *teaspoon paprika*
 ½ *teaspoon cumin*
 ¼ *teaspoon savory*
 ½ *teaspoon seasoned salt*

In a colander, wash beans and remove any bad ones or stones. Put beans in a 4-quart soup pot with 2 quarts water; cover and soak overnight. (For a quick soak, boil 2 minutes, remove from heat; cover and let stand 1 hour.) Pour off water and rinse beans. Add 2 quarts fresh water, ham bone, onion, celery, bay leaf, garlic, and parsley; cover and simmer for 2 hours. Add remaining seasonings; cover and cook 1 hour. Check for doneness; beans are fully cooked if center is tender when pinched. Remove ham bone, cool and cut off all lean meat; discard bone and fat. Slice meat across the grain in one-half-inch pieces and return to pot.

SERVES 6.

This recipe is a homemade version of the Bean Soup kits sold at our Cranbrook Gardens annual plant sales.

## SPLIT PEA SOUP

 2 *tablespoons olive oil*
 1 *cup trimmed, chopped celery*
 1 *cup chopped carrots*
 1 *medium onion, chopped*
 8 *cups water*
 1 *pound dry green split peas*
 1 *teaspoon dried thyme (or 2 teaspoons fresh)*
 ¼ *cup finely chopped parsley (or 2 tablespoons dried)*
 ½ *teaspoon ground pepper*
1 ½ *tablespoons chicken flavored instant bouillon granules*

Heat olive oil in Dutch oven. Add celery, carrots, and onion and sauté until crisp-tender. Stir in water, peas, thyme, parsley, and pepper. Heat to boiling; reduce heat and simmer, covered, for 50 minutes or until thick. Sprinkle in bouillon granules and stir thoroughly until dissolved.

SERVES 8.

A delicious soup which appeals to all ages. It's high in fiber and very low in cholesterol.

## STEAK SOUP

2  pounds ground round
½  cup butter
1  cup flour
4  cups water
¼  cup beef bouillon granules
½  teaspoon ground black pepper
1  large onion, diced
2-3  carrots, chopped
2-3  ribs celery, sliced
2  cups undrained canned chopped tomatoes
20  ounces frozen mixed vegetables

In a 4-quart saucepan, brown ground beef, drain, remove, and set aside. Melt butter in saucepan, then remove from heat. Add flour, whisking until smooth. Return to heat. Gradually add water and continue to whisk. Add bouillon granules, black pepper, onion, carrots, celery, tomatoes, and browned beef. Simmer 2-3 hours, adding more water if broth is too thick. Add the frozen vegetables and cook 15 minutes or less. Remove from heat when vegetables are still crunchy.

SERVES 8.

**A thick, rich beef soup with crunchy vegetables.**

## POTATO-CARROT POTAGE

2  cups diced onions
½  cup butter or margarine
1½  cups chopped celery
4  cups peeled, thinly sliced carrots
8  cups peeled, diced potatoes
2  quarts chicken broth, seasoned
  GARNISH:
1  cup heavy cream or sour cream
4  tablespoons chopped chives

In a 6-quart soup pot, sauté onions in hot butter or margarine for 3 minutes over medium heat. Add celery and continue to sauté 3 additional minutes. Add carrots, potatoes, and chicken broth. Bring to a boil, reduce temperature and simmer for 1 hour or until potatoes and carrots are very soft. Purée about one-third of soup in a blender or food processor. Return purée to soup pot to thicken broth. At serving time, pour 1 tablespoon heavy cream in each bowl or add a dollop of sour cream and sprinkle with chopped chives.

SERVES 10-12.

Did you ever see a pair of pants

Hanging from a vine?

They belong to the wild cucumber

So that pair's not mine!

# SALADS

## COLD BEEF SALAD MEADOWBROOK

1  whole beef tenderloin (2-2½ pounds), cooked
   and chilled
1  pound boiling potatoes
2  tablespoons dry vermouth
4  tablespoons white wine vinegar
2  teaspoons dry mustard
½  teaspoon salt
¾  cup olive oil
   ground black pepper
2-3  tablespoons chopped fresh herbs
   (parsley, basil, chives, tarragon)
1  hard-cooked egg, sliced
1  purple onion, thinly sliced
   several leaves of Boston lettuce
1  tomato, quartered
2-3  cooked beets, sliced and chilled
½  pound green beans, cooked and chilled
3  mushrooms, sliced

Boil potatoes until just tender. Drain, peel and slice. While still warm, add dry vermouth. To prepare dressing, whisk vinegar, mustard and salt together, then slowly add oil and season with pepper and herbs. Pour one-third of dressing over potatoes, reserve remainder. Prepare egg and vegetables; slice beef thinly. Wrap ingredients separately in resealable containers, if transporting to a picnic. Assemble salad just before serving: line platter with lettuce leaves and cover with potato salad; arrange egg and vegetables around platter; place beef slices on top. Pour reserved dressing over salad. Serve with a crusty loaf of French bread.

SERVES 4-5.

Picnic baskets on the lovely grounds of Meadowbrook's outdoor theatre in Rochester, Michigan, often hold the makings for this salad.

# ANNIVERSARY CHICKEN AND WILD RICE SALAD

SALAD:

| | |
|---|---|
| 4 | cups shredded cooked chicken |
| 1 | cup wild rice |
| 1 | teaspoon salt |
| 7 | ounces marinated artichoke hearts, drained |
| 4 | ribs celery, julienned |
| 7 | scallions, cross-cut, finely sliced |
| 2 | carrots, diced |
| 8-10 | radishes, thinly sliced |
| 1 | onion, diced |
| 1 | head cauliflower, cut in small florets |
| ¼ | cup finely chopped parsley |
| 1 | cup pine nuts or pecans |
| | dressing (recipe follows) |

GARNISH:

| | |
|---|---|
| 1 | sweet red pepper, sliced |
| 6 | ounces pitted black olives, drained |

DRESSING:

| | |
|---|---|
| 1 | cup mayonnaise |
| 2 | tablespoons curry powder |
| 1 | cup olive oil |
| ⅓ | cup vinegar |
| 1 | tablespoon Dijon mustard |
| 1 | garlic clove, finely minced |
| 1 | teaspoon salt |
| | ground black pepper |

Mix together above salad dressing ingredients in a quart jar. Shake to blend.

SERVES 12-16.

Rinse wild rice twice in a fine mesh strainer. In a saucepan, add rice and salt to 3 cups water and cook, covered, for 40 minutes or until tender. In a large bowl, combine chicken, rice, vegetables, and nuts. Toss. Stir in dressing, cover bowl and refrigerate overnight. At serving time, mound rice salad in a shallow bowl and garnish with sliced red pepper and black olives.

**Simply irresistible! The perfect main event for a summer buffet. Add a plate of marinated vegetables, a tossed mixed greens salad, and a fresh fruit melange.**

## GATEHOUSE CHICKEN PASTA SALAD

DRESSING:
- ⅔ cup olive oil
- 5 tablespoons red wine vinegar
- ¼ cup chopped fresh basil leaves
  (or 2 tablespoons dried)
- 3 tablespoons grated Parmesan cheese
- 1 tablespoon fresh oregano
  (or ½ tablespoon dried)
- 1 teaspoon salt
- ½ teaspoon ground black pepper

SALAD:
- 4 cups cooked, cubed chicken
- 8 ounces rotelle pasta, cooked, rinsed,
  and drained
- 1 red pepper, sliced thin
- 1 green pepper, sliced thin
- 1½ cups broccoli florets, cooked 2 minutes,
  rinsed, chilled
- ½ cup sliced, pitted black olives
- 1 cup cherry tomatoes, sliced in half
- ½ cup mayonnaise (or mayonnaise-base
  salad dressing)

Prepare dressing first. In a blender, mix together olive oil, red wine vinegar, basil leaves, cheese, oregano, salt and pepper; set aside.

In a large bowl, combine chicken, pasta, and vegetables; toss salad with oil and vinegar dressing. Refrigerate 8 hours or overnight. At serving time toss salad with one-half cup mayonnaise.

SERVES 6-8.

## CLASSIC CHICKEN SALAD

- 3 tablespoons butter
- 1 cup chopped pecans
- 4 cups cooked cubed chicken breast
- 1 cup mayonnaise (or equal parts mayonnaise
  and mayonnaise-base salad dressing)
- 2 cups seedless grapes, cut in half
- ½ cup chopped celery (optional)
  salt and pepper to taste
  lettuce or radicchio

Sauté pecans in melted butter; drain and mix with chicken. Add mayonnaise, grapes, celery, salt and pepper; mix well and chill. Serve on a platter lined with lettuce leaves or radicchio.

SERVES 4.

A recipe collection is not complete without our updated version of the "classic" chicken salad.

## CURRIED CHICKEN SALAD

4 *chicken breasts, split*
*chicken broth for poaching*
1 *cup mayonnaise*
½ *cup plain yogurt*
1½ *tablespoons curry powder*
¼ *cup chutney*
1 *cup chopped scallions*
1 *cup chopped celery*
1½ *cups seedless grapes, halved if large*
1 *cup cashews, toasted lightly*
  GARNISH:
  *melon wedges*
  *grape clusters*

Poach the chicken breasts in broth until tender. Cool in broth, remove and cut into bite-size pieces. In a bowl, whisk together mayonnaise, yogurt, curry powder, and chutney. Add the chicken to the curry dressing with the scallion, celery, and grapes. Toss until well combined; chill thoroughly. Mound the salad on a chilled large platter, sprinkle with cashews. Garnish the platter with melon wedges and small grape clusters.

SERVES 8.

## RAINBOW SHRIMP SALAD

1 *cup cooked brown rice*
1 *pound fresh shrimp, cooked, peeled,*
  *and deveined*
½ *cup chopped green pepper*
1 *small onion, finely minced*
½ *cup sliced green olives*
1 *cup diced cauliflower*
  *juice of ½ lemon*
½ *cup mayonnaise*
  *salt and pepper to taste*
  *lettuce leaves*

In a large bowl, combine all ingredients. Refrigerate 3-4 hours; toss occasionally. Serve on a bed of lettuce.

SERVES 6.

## Salad Niçoise

2  tablespoons red wine vinegar
6  tablespoons olive oil
2  teaspoons Dijon mustard
   salt and pepper
1  small garlic clove, slightly crushed
1  head Bibb or Boston lettuce, rinsed,
   ribs removed
2  cups cooked, quartered new potatoes
2  cups cooked, cut green beans (1-inch pieces)
6  ounces tuna chunks (preferably packed
   in olive oil)
3  tomatoes, cut into wedges
3  hard-boiled eggs, cut into wedges
   Garnish:
6-8  black olives
6  anchovy filets
1  teaspoon capers

In a small bowl, whisk together vinegar, olive oil, and mustard. Season with salt and pepper and set aside. Rub a shallow salad bowl or deep platter with crushed garlic clove. Arrange lettuce leaves along bottom and sides of bowl. Arrange cooled potatoes around the edge of dish. Heap the green beans in the center of the potatoes. Drain tuna chunks on green beans and decorate with tomato and hard-boiled egg wedges. Drizzle vinaigrette dressing over bowl. Garnish with olives, anchovies, and capers. Toss salad at the table.

Serves 6.

**This typically French dish makes a refreshing luncheon entrée on a warm summer day.**

## Ross' Caesar Salad

1  small clove garlic, minced
⅓  cup olive oil
   thick-sliced French or Italian bread
   (for croutons)
2  tablespoons butter
1  pound romaine lettuce
1  large egg, very fresh, room temperature
¾  teaspoon salt
¼  teaspoon fresh ground pepper
3  tablespoons fresh lemon juice
2  teaspoons Worcestershire sauce
¼  cup grated Parmesan cheese

Mix garlic and olive oil in small cup. Allow to set at room temperature for several hours. To prepare croutons, trim and cube several one-half-inch-thick slices of French or Italian bread to make 1½ cups. In heavy 10-inch skillet, melt 2 tablespoons butter. Add cubes and brown over medium-low heat 3-5 minutes, tossing constantly. Set aside. Tear romaine in bite-size pieces into large salad bowl; chill. Before serving, coddle egg in a bowl of boiling water one minute, then rinse under cold water to stop cooking. Toss romaine with garlic-oil mixture, salt and pepper. Break egg into middle of greens. Sprinkle greens with lemon juice and Worcestershire, then toss well. Add croutons and cheese, toss lightly and serve.

Serves 6.

## Couscous Salad with Currants and Pine Nuts

   3  tablespoons unsalted butter
   ⅛  teaspoon powdered saffron
1½  cups chicken broth
1½  cups couscous
1½  cups diced celery
   ⅔  cup dried currants (soaked in hot water
       for 15 minutes and drained)
   ⅓  cup thinly sliced scallions
   ⅓  cup pine nuts, lightly toasted
   ¼  cup minced parsley
   ¼  cup fresh lemon juice
   ¼  teaspoon ground cinnamon
   ½  cup olive oil

 In a large skillet, melt butter with saffron over medium heat, stirring; add broth, bring liquid to a boil. Stir in couscous; cover and remove from heat. Let mixture stand 4 minutes and transfer to a ceramic or glass bowl; break up lumps with a fork. Add celery, currants, scallions, pine nuts, and parsley; toss to combine. In a small bowl, whisk lemon juice and cinnamon, add oil in stream, whisking continuously. Drizzle dressing over salad, toss and season with salt and pepper. Chill, covered, for 2-3 hours before serving.

Serves 6-8.

## Vegetable-Fruit Pasta Salad

   1  head broccoli, trimmed and diced
   1  head cauliflower, trimmed and diced
4-6  carrots, sliced
   1  red onion
   1  pint strawberries
   1  large pear
   3  ounces black pitted olives, drained
   8  ounces sliced water chestnuts, drained
12  ounces mixed vegetable rotini pasta
   2  chicken breasts, cooked, cooled, and diced
       (optional)
       Sweet and Sour or Honey French salad dressing

Boil water in pan and remove from heat. Add broccoli, cauliflower, and carrots; blanch for about 5 minutes; drain and cool. Slice red onion lengthwise; hull and halve strawberries; cut pear in pieces. Cook pasta as directed and cool. Mix all ingredients together and toss in a large bowl with salad dressing. Chill thoroughly before serving.

Serves 8-10.

## Bloomfield Winter Salad

DRESSING:

¼ cup sugar
1 teaspoon salt
1 teaspoon paprika
1 teaspoon dry mustard
¼ teaspoon pepper
¼ cup fresh lemon juice
1 teaspoon celery seed
1 tablespoon diced onion
1 large or 2 medium cloves of garlic
2 tablespoons honey
¾ cup light vegetable oil

Combine all ingredients in a blender and mix until smooth. Makes 1½ cups of salad dressing. Extra dressing, stored in the refrigerator, keeps for weeks.

SALAD:

1 head romaine lettuce, washed, dried, torn into pieces
2 oranges, peeled and cut into sections without pith
1 grapefruit, peeled and cut into sections without pith
   garlic salt, to taste
   salt and pepper, to taste
1 red onion, peeled and thinly sliced
1 ripe avocado, peeled and sliced

Toss together romaine lettuce, oranges, and grapefruit. Sprinkle salad with a little garlic salt, salt and pepper. Toss with salad dressing. Arrange red onion rings and avocado wedges on top of salad.

SERVES 6.

The salad dressing makes this salad special!

## MICHIGAN APPLE-CHERRY TOSS

3   medium-size, tart, crisp Michigan apples
     (Jonathan, Snow, MacIntosh)
1   tablespoon fresh lemon juice
1   cup thinly sliced, diagonal cut celery
½   cup dried Michigan cherries
½   cup broken walnut meats
½   cup sweetened mayonnaise-base salad dressing
     Bibb lettuce leaves

Peel, core, and cube apples (3 cups) into a 1½-quart bowl. If green Granny Smith's are used, skin may be left on for color contrast. Sprinkle on lemon juice and stir to prevent discoloring. Add celery, cherries, and walnuts; mix together. Add dressing and combine thoroughly. Cover and refrigerate for 1 hour; cherries will start to plump. Arrange each serving on a whole lettuce leaf.

SERVES 4-6.

## JUMP FOR JOY JELLO SALAD

 6   ounces lemon flavored gelatin
2⅔   cups boiling water
20   ounces canned crushed pineapple, undrained
 1   cup chopped walnuts
 1   cup chopped celery
12   ounces evaporated milk
     GARNISH:
     clusters of red or purple grapes

In a large bowl, dissolve gelatin in boiling water. Cool, then add pineapple, nuts, celery, and evaporated milk. Stir to combine. Pour into an oiled 6-cup ring mold. Chill until firm. Invert mold onto a serving plate and fill center of ring with grapes.

SERVES 12.

Some things never change. The popularity of gelatin molds like this one has endured for generations.

## FREEZIN' COLE SLAW

1   *large head cabbage, trimmed and cored*
1   *large carrot*
½  *green pepper, minced*
1   *teaspoon salt*
1   *cup cider vinegar*
¼  *cup water*
1   *teaspoon celery seed*
1   *teaspoon Dijon mustard*
2   *cups sugar*

Shred cabbage and carrot by hand or in a food processor. Toss together in a large bowl with green pepper and salt. In a saucepan, bring to a boil vinegar, water, celery seed, mustard, and sugar. Boil for one minute and cool. Pour cooled dressing over vegetables, tossing well. Freeze until needed. Drain well before serving.

SERVES 10-12.

**Great to keep on hand for impromptu cookouts!**

## LIMA BEAN LOVER'S SALAD

10   *ounces fresh or frozen baby Lima beans*
8   *large mushrooms, sliced*
4   *green onions, sliced*
2   *tablespoons finely chopped parsley*
½  *teaspoon dried oregano*
¼  *cup oil and vinegar salad dressing*
    *salt and pepper*
    GARNISH:
8-10  *pimento slices*

In a medium saucepan, cook Lima beans until just tender. Drain and rinse in cold water. In a medium bowl, toss together beans, mushrooms, onions, and herbs. Stir dressing into vegetables. Season to taste with salt and pepper. Decorate salad with pimento slices and serve immediately at room temperature, or may be prepared up to 24 hours in advance, refrigerated, and served chilled.

SERVES 4-6.

## AVOCADO-CELERY SALAD

1 cup salad oil
6 tablespoons white wine or apple cider vinegar
¼ cup sugar
½ teaspoon dry mustard
1⅛ teaspoons celery seed
2½ tablespoons grated onion
1½ teaspoons salt or to taste
4-5 ripe avocados
1 bunch celery (7-8 stalks)
GARNISH:
10 large radicchio leaves
2 medium red bell peppers, seeded
and sliced into rings

In a lidded jar or bowl, combine oil, vinegar, sugar, mustard, celery seed, onion, and salt. Shake or whisk to blend. Peel and pit avocados. Place in a medium bowl, add the dressing and mash the avocados with a fork. Trim and peel the celery stalks, cut into bite-size pieces and add to the avocado mixture. Cover and chill. To serve, spoon salad into individual radicchio cups and garnish with red pepper rings.

SERVES 10.

**A very tasty, very different salad.**

## FRESH ASPARAGUS SALAD

1 pound fresh asparagus, trimmed
½ cup cooked red kidney beans
(if canned, rinse and drain)
5 green onions, sliced (white part only)
DRESSING:
½ cup extra virgin olive oil
2 tablespoons red wine vinegar
1½ teaspoons mustard
½ teaspoon dried basil
salt and pepper to taste

Steam or boil asparagus until just tender. Drain, rinse with cold water, and cut into 2-inch pieces. In a medium bowl, gently toss together asparagus, beans, and onions. Set aside. In a blender or small bowl, mix together olive oil, vinegar, mustard, basil, and salt and pepper. Add enough dressing to asparagus salad to moisten and toss again. Serve at room temperature or chilled.

SERVES 4.

**When the tender asparagus stalks are plentiful, this salad is a delightful way to serve them.**

## BLUE CHEESE SALAD DRESSING

¼ pound blue cheese, crumbled
1 clove garlic, crushed
1 pint sour cream
¼ cup mayonnaise
2 tablespoons lemon juice
  salt and pepper to taste

 Mix all ingredients with wire whisk or electric hand mixer; chill. Spoon over mixed salad or a wedge of lettuce.

MAKES 1½ PINTS.

**This is also very good as a dip with fresh vegetables.**

## CELERY SEED SALAD DRESSING

½ cup cider vinegar (not white distilled)
½ medium onion, quartered
1 teaspoon salt
1 teaspoon dry mustard
½ cup sugar
1 cup salad oil
2 tablespoons celery seed

Mix together in blender vinegar, onion, salt, dry mustard, and sugar. With blender running, slowly add oil and celery seed.

MAKES 1½ CUPS.

The sun is shining so very hot!

It's not as hot as a boiling pot.

The roast is roasting, the cookies bake

All food is cooked for our tummy's sake.

My tummy's always good to me—

It helps me run, it helps me see.

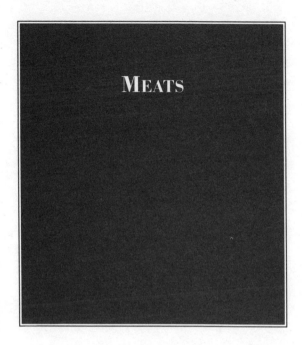

# MEATS

## KANSAS CITY BRISKET

4½-5  pounds fresh brisket of beef
       salt to taste
  ½    teaspoon pepper
  ½    cup instant minced onion
  ½    teaspoon celery salt
  ½    teaspoon garlic powder
  ½    cup Worcestershire sauce
 1¾    ounces liquid smoke
  1    batch of Aunt Jessie's Barbeque Sauce
       (recipe follows)

AUNT JESSIE'S BARBEQUE SAUCE:
2½  cups catsup
 3  tablespoons margarine
 3  tablespoons sugar
 3  tablespoons brown sugar
 ¼  teaspoon oregano powder
 ¼  teaspoon ground cumin
 ¼  teaspoon garlic powder
 1  teaspoon liquid smoke

Line an 11 x 14-inch casserole with a large (about 30-inch) sheet of heavy duty aluminum foil. Place the brisket on the foil fat side up. Sprinkle with all of the above ingredients except the barbeque sauce. Close the foil around the brisket, sealing the top edges together and rolling down. Marinate in the refrigerator overnight. Next morning put the foil wrapped brisket in a 250 degree oven and bake for 5 hours. Allow to cool and skim off fat. Reserve about 1 cup of the remaining liquid. Slice the meat very thin across the grain and return it along with the reserved liquid to the clean casserole. Completely cover brisket with barbeque sauce basting it between slices. Reheat and serve as an entrée or accompanied with poppy seed sandwich rolls.

Mix together and bring to a boil. Cover and let cool. Great on beef, chicken or pork.

SERVES 8-10.

This is a cherished family recipe from Kansas City where barbeque is taken very seriously!

## LONDON BROIL ON THE GRILL

1½ pounds flank steak, London broil, or skirt steak
    MARINADE:
  2 tablespoons oil
  2 tablespoons fresh lemon juice
  ½ cup soy sauce
  2 tablespoons firmly packed brown sugar
  ¼ teaspoon pepper
  1 clove garlic, minced
  1 tablespoon instant minced onion
  1 teaspoon ground ginger

 Score flank steak lightly in a diagonal pattern. Blend marinade ingredients. Pour over meat, cover and refrigerate overnight. Let stand at room temperature 1 hour before grilling. Grill or broil 6 minutes on each side. Baste after turning. Slice in strips diagonally across the grain.

SERVES 4.

**Serve with fruit compote, pasta salad, and crunchy bread for a casual barbecue.**

## BEEF AND MANGO CURRY

  4 tablespoons butter
  2 tablespoons oil
  2 pounds round steak, trimmed and
    cut into ¾-inch cubes
  2 garlic cloves, minced
  2 large onions, finely chopped
  2 tablespoons curry powder (or to taste)
  1 cup dry white wine
  1 cup water
  2 chicken bouillon cubes
  1 pound canned sliced mangoes
    salt and pepper to taste
  3 teaspoons cornstarch

Heat butter and oil in a pan; add one-quarter of the meat and cook quickly over medium-high heat until all sides of the meat are dark golden brown. Remove from pan and repeat browning process in batches with remaining meat. Add garlic and onion to pan, sauté gently over medium heat until onion is lightly golden. Add curry powder, sauté 1 minute longer. Return meat to pan. Add wine, water and crumbled bouillon cubes. Drain mangoes, reserving ½ cup liquid. Purée mangoes and reserved liquid in blender (or push through a sieve). Add to meat. Season with salt and pepper. Bring to boil, reduce heat, simmer covered 1½ hours. Blend cornstarch with ¼ cup water, add to meat mixture and stir until mixture thickens. Serve with rice. This recipe may be made in advance and reheated. (Note: Canned, sliced mangoes can be found in any Asian grocery store.)

SERVES 4-6.

**Here velvety, sweet mangoes add a pleasant surprise to a seemingly traditional dish.**

## BEEF-VEGETABLE STIR-FRY

1    pound top round steak
1½   cups cut broccoli (1-inch pieces)
3    medium carrots, diagonally sliced
1    teaspoon cornstarch
1    teaspoon salt
½    teaspoon sugar
2    tablespoons soy sauce
2    tablespoons dry sherry
2    tablespoons cooking oil
1    medium onion, sliced thin
1    cup frozen peas, thawed
½    cup thinly sliced water chestnuts, drained
½    cup sliced bamboo shoots

 Partially freeze beef, slice very thinly across the grain into bite-sized strips. Parboil broccoli and carrots, covered, for 2 minutes; drain. Mix cornstarch, salt, and sugar; blend in soy sauce and sherry. Set aside. Preheat a wok over high heat; add oil, heat. Stir-fry broccoli, carrots, and onion for 2 minutes. Remove from wok. Add more oil if necessary. Add half the beef to wok, stir-fry 2-3 minutes. Remove and stir-fry remainder of beef. Return all beef to wok, add peas, water chestnuts, and bamboo shoots. Add soy sauce mixture. Cook and stir until thickened and bubbly. Return broccoli, carrots, and onion to wok; cover and heat 1 minute. Serve with rice or fried noodles.

SERVES 4-6.

## DANISH CHILI

3    tablespoons butter or margarine
1½   cups thinly sliced onions
1    cup chopped green pepper
2    pounds lean sirloin steak, cubed
28   ounces canned tomatoes
½    cup dry red wine
1    clove garlic, finely minced
1    teaspoon salt
½    teaspoon pepper
1    teaspoon oregano
1    teaspoon paprika
4    tablespoons chili powder (or to taste)
½    teaspoon caraway seeds
21   ounces canned dark red kidney beans

 Melt butter in a large saucepan, sauté onion and peppers on medium heat until translucent and soft. Add beef and continue cooking until no longer pink. Add remaining ingredients except beans. Simmer uncovered 1½ hours. Add beans, continue to simmer for 30 minutes.

SERVES 6-8.

**Full-bodied, chunky beef chili becomes Danish with a touch of caraway.**

## PICADILLO

2   pounds ground round
1   tablespoon vegetable oil
3   garlic cloves, minced
2   large onions, chopped
1   cup tomato sauce
1¼  cups red wine
⅛   teaspoon oregano
1½  cups golden raisins, soaked in water until
     plump
½   cup sliced pimento-stuffed olives
2   green peppers, seeded and chopped

Brown the beef in oil for 3-5 minutes. Add the garlic, onions, tomato sauce, wine, and oregano. Simmer for 15 minutes. Drain the raisins and add with olives and green pepper to the beef. Simmer 5 minutes. Serve on a bed of rice.

SERVES 6.

**An unusual version of the classic picadillo which originated in the Phillipine Islands.**

## EAST INDIAN MEAT LOAF

2   pounds ground beef chuck
1   teaspoon salt
¼   teaspoon pepper
½   teaspoon curry powder
2   eggs
½   teaspoon garlic powder
2   tablespoons instant minced onion (or 4 table-
     spoons minced fresh onion)
2   large apples, peeled, cored, and finely diced
     (MacIntosh or Jonathan)
½   cup orange juice
⅓   cup chopped chutney

Preheat oven to 350 degrees. Mix beef, salt, pepper, curry, eggs, garlic, onion, apples, and orange juice together in a bowl. Shape the mixture into a loaf and place in a shallow baking pan lined with foil. Bake for 1 hour. Remove from oven and drain fat. Spread chutney on top of the loaf and return to oven for an additional 10 minutes.

SERVES 4-6.

## HOMESTYLE TACOS

**SAUCE:**

| | |
|---|---|
| 2 | cups canned tomatoes or tomato sauce |
| 6 | tablespoons chili sauce |
| 3 | tablespoons vinegar |
| 1 | tablespoon grated onion or minced onion |
| 1 | clove garlic, minced |
| 2 | teaspoons dry mustard |
| ¾ | teaspoon salt |
| ½ | teaspoon sugar |
| ½ | teaspoon chili powder |
| ¼ | teaspoon cumin |
| | dash of red pepper |

**FILLING:**

| | |
|---|---|
| 1 | pound ground beef |
| 1 | medium onion, finely chopped |
| 1 | medium tomato, chopped |
| 1 | teaspoon chili powder |
| 1 | teaspoon oregano |
| ½ | teaspoon salt |
| ¼ | teaspoon cumin |
| | dash of pepper |
| 10 | tortillas or taco shells |
| 2 | cups shredded lettuce |
| 2 | chopped tomatoes |
| ¼ | pound grated Cheddar cheese |

To make sauce, mix all the ingredients in a medium pan and bring to a boil. Reduce heat and simmer until thickened, about 30 minutes.

In a skillet, brown meat and onions together. Add chopped tomato, chili powder, oregano, salt, cumin, and pepper. Let simmer while warming tortillas or taco shells. Put a little of the meat filling in a taco shell and add sauce, shredded lettuce, chopped tomatoes, and grated cheese. Serve with the sauce.

SERVES 4-5.

**The filling recipe simply converts into a taco salad. Just garnish it with avocado and taco chips. Serve the sauce on the side.**

## SIX LITTLE LEMON LOAVES

1½  pounds ground round
¼  cup fresh lemon juice
½  cup water
1  egg, slightly beaten
4  slices stale bread, finely diced
¼  cup chopped onion
1  teaspoon salt
¼  teaspoon celery salt
⅛  teaspoon ground ginger
½  cup catsup
⅓  cup brown sugar, firmly packed
1  teaspoon dry mustard
¼  teaspoon ground cloves
¼  teaspoon ground allspice
6  thin lemon slices

Preheat oven to 350 degrees. Combine beef, lemon juice, water, egg, bread, onion, salt, celery salt, and ginger; form into six small loaves. Bake in greased baking pan for 15 minutes. Meanwhile, combine catsup, brown sugar, mustard, cloves, and allspice. After 15 minutes of baking, put half of the sauce on the loaves, top each with a lemon slice, and bake 15 minutes more. Then put the rest of the topping on the loaves, bake 15 more minutes, or 45 minutes in all.

SERVES 6.

**A refreshing change from the standard American meatloaf.**

## VEAL PICCATA

4  veal cutlets (1-1½ pounds)
   salt and pepper to taste
½  cup flour
3  teaspoons olive oil
2  teaspoons minced green onion
¼  cup dry vermouth (or dry white wine)
4-8  tablespoons butter or margarine
   juice of ½ lemon
1  tablespoon capers
   GARNISH:
1  tablespoon chopped Italian parsley

Pound the veal cutlets wafer thin. Salt and pepper and dust with flour. Brown in oil on both sides. Remove veal and keep warm. Add minced green onions and vermouth. Boil until the vermouth is almost evaporated. Add butter or margarine, lemon juice, and capers; stir with whisk to form sauce. Pour over veal and serve with rice. Garnish with chopped parsley.

SERVES 4.

**The flavor of this classic Italian specialty improves when made with a select extra virgin olive oil.**

## Veal Italiano

2 pounds boned shoulder of veal, cut in chunks
⅓ cup flour
½-1 pound mushrooms
6 tablespoons butter or margarine, divided
1 teaspoon pepper
1 tablespoon garlic, minced in 1 teaspoon salt
½ teaspoon dried thyme
1 tablespoon chopped parsley
1 cup tomato purée
1 cup chicken stock
½ cup Madeira wine (dry)
2 tablespoons lemon juice
GARNISH:
grated Parmesan cheese

Trim veal chunks. Place flour and meat in a paper bag and shake until all chunks are coated evenly. Slice mushrooms and sauté in a large skillet with two tablespoons of butter. Transfer to oven casserole with close-fitting cover. Add more butter to skillet and brown chunks of meat in batches. Transfer to oven casserole with mushrooms. Add remaining ingredients to skillet and deglaze the pan. Pour over meat and mushrooms. Cover and bake at 350 degrees one hour or until tender. Taste for seasoning and correct if necessary. Garnish with grated Parmesan cheese. Serve with rice or egg noodles.

SERVES 6.

**Beef, pork, or chicken can easily be substituted for the veal; just adjust the baking time.**

## Veal Paprikás

1 medium onion, diced
3 tablespoons olive oil
2 pounds veal stew meat, trimmed, cut into 1-inch cubes
2 tablespoons tomato paste
½ cup chicken stock, lightly seasoned
1 tablespoon paprika
ground black pepper
2-3 tablespoons sour cream

In a 4-quart Dutch oven, sauté onions in olive oil. When lightly golden, remove with a slotted spoon. Add veal cubes and brown lightly. Return onions to pot, add stock, tomato paste, and paprika. Stir. Bring mixture to a boil over medium-high heat, reduce temperature, cover surface of stew with a sheet of aluminum foil and simmer about 25 minutes or until tender. Add sour cream, and season with black pepper. If sauce is very thin, add 1 tablespoon of cornstarch mixed with 1 tablespoon of water, stirring over medium heat until thickened. Serve with egg noodles or rice.

SERVES 4.

## Veal Parmesan Roast

2 eggs
2 tablespoons water
½ cup freshly grated Parmesan cheese
½ cup seasoned bread crumbs
1 teaspoon salt
2½-3 pounds veal brisket, fat trimmed
⅓ cup oil
15 ounces marinara sauce or any good tomato
sauce
1 pound fresh mushrooms, sautéed in small
amount of butter
6 ounces mozzarella cheese, sliced

 Beat eggs with water in large flat plate. On paper towel, mix Parmesan with bread crumbs and salt. Wipe veal with damp towel. Dredge in egg, then crumbs and allow to rest for ½ hour. Heat oil in skillet. Brown in hot oil until golden on both sides, being careful not to burn. Drain off excess oil. Reduce heat to low, cover and simmer meat in its own juices until fork-tender (about 1½ hours). Remove to shallow casserole, cover with half the sauce, then cover with foil. (May be made, up to this point, one or two days before serving.) Preheat oven to 350 degrees. Place foil-covered dish in oven for about 25-30 minutes, heating only until hot. Remove foil and spoon on sautéed mushrooms, moistening with sauce. Cover all with slices of mozzarella and rest of sauce. Bake uncovered for 10 minutes. Place under broiler to completely melt cheese and brown slightly. Watch carefully! Slice into serving pieces and cover with accumulated sauce remaining in pan if desired.

SERVES 6.

Although this recipe serves 6, plan it as an entrée for 4 to ensure leftovers. They are well worth the wait. For a luncheon sandwich, cover veal slices with reheated sauce.

## BUTTERFLIED LEG OF LAMB

5-6 pound leg of lamb, butterflied and trimmed
4  tablespoons olive oil
1  teaspoon crumbled rosemary
   salt and pepper
   juice and zest from 1 large orange
½  cup butter
3  tablespoons Dijon mustard

Have butcher bone and butterfly the leg of lamb. Rub both sides of lamb with olive oil and sprinkle with the rosemary, salt and pepper to taste. Place lamb meat side up in a 9 x 11-inch roasting pan. Broil 6 inches from the heat for 10-20 minutes depending on personal preference for rare, medium, or well done. Turn lamb and broil for another 10-15 minutes. Prepare sauce by heating the orange juice, zest, and butter in a small saucepan. Simmer mixture for 2 minutes. Remove from heat and whisk the mustard into the sauce. Spread the warm sauce over the lamb just before serving. To serve, slice lamb across the grain of the meat.

SERVES 6-8.

## MINTED LAMB LUNCHEON

1  pound lean ground lamb
¼  cup crumbled dried mint leaves
2  tablespoons chopped fresh parsley
1  egg
6  (2-inch) soda crackers, crushed
1  cup marinara sauce
4  cups cooked wild or basmatia rice

In a 2-quart bowl, combine ground lamb, mint, parsley, egg, and crackers. When well blended, form mixture into balls the size of walnuts. Put balls in a large frying pan over medium heat and turn gently until browned on all sides. Drain off fat and pour tomato sauce over meat. Lower heat, cover, and simmer for 30 minutes. Serve over cooked rice.

SERVES 4.

A savory luncheon favorite of herbal authority, Marian Bates.

## RACK OF LAMB GENGHIS KHAN

3  lamb racks (8 ribs each), trimmed
   and silverskin removed
   lamb marinade (recipe follows)
1  cup hoisin sauce

 Place the lamb and marinade in a plastic bag, tie, and place in refrigerator for 48 hours, turning occasionally. Remove lamb from marinade and let stand at room temperature 1 hour before cooking. Brush with hoisin sauce. Place lamb on rack in shallow roasting pan and roast in hot oven, 450 degrees, for 15-25 minutes for rare lamb, depending on the size of the racks, or longer for a greater degree of doneness. Let rest for 6-7 minutes before carving.

LAMB MARINADE:
1    cup finely chopped onions
2    tablespoons minced garlic
3    tablespoons lemon juice
½    cup honey
3    tablespoons curry powder
1½   teaspoons ground cayenne pepper
2    teaspoons Coleman's mustard powder
2    teaspoons ground black pepper
2    tablespoons salt
1    cup water

Combine all ingredients.

SERVES 6.

The Lark Restaurant
West Bloomfield, Michigan

This is a house specialty at the four-star Lark Restaurant in West Bloomfield, Michigan. Each rack of lamb is numbered and is served with a numbered certificate.

## COUNTRY HAM CASSEROLE

10½ ounces canned cream of mushroom soup,
    undiluted
 ½ cup milk
 1 teaspoon instant minced onions
 2 teaspoons Dijon mustard
 1 cup dairy sour cream
   butter or margarine for sautéing
 ¼ cup chopped green pepper
 ½ pound sliced fresh mushrooms
 2 tablespoons pine nuts (optional)
 ¼ cup sliced ripe olives
 4 ounces egg noodles
 2 cups julienned cooked ham (1-inch strips)
 ¼ cup dry bread crumbs
1½ tablespoons butter or margarine, melted
 2 tablespoons grated fresh Parmesan cheese

Preheat oven to 350 degrees. In a small saucepan, over medium heat, combine soup and milk stirring until smooth. Add onion, mustard, and sour cream. Blend well. Sauté green pepper and mushrooms until tender. Combine with sauce and add pine nuts and ripe olives. Cook egg noodles according to package directions and drain. Combine noodles, sauce, and ham. Place in a greased 1½-quart casserole. Toss bread crumbs with butter and spread on top of casserole. Sprinkle with Parmesan cheese. Bake uncovered 25 minutes or until golden brown. Can be made ahead, frozen, and baked later.

SERVES 6.

A casserole designed "to go"—to pot luck meals. Tastes just as good warm as hot from the oven.

## CHINESE SPARERIBS

3½ pounds pork spareribs, cut into 2-inch pieces
 2 large onions, sliced
 ½ cup brown sugar, packed
 ½ cup vinegar
 1 tablespoon soy sauce
20 ounces canned pineapple chunks in natural
    juice, drained and ⅔ cup juice reserved
 ⅓ cup water
 ½ teaspoon salt
 ⅛ teaspoon black pepper
 1 tablespoon cornstarch mixed with 1 tablespoon
    water
 1 green pepper, sliced in wide strips
 2 large fresh tomatoes, cut into wedges

Have butcher saw racks of spareribs crosswise into 2-inch pieces. Place ribs close together on broiler rack. (If desired, sprinkle with added salt and pepper.) Broil, turning once, until brown on both sides. In Dutch oven, or any large heavy pan which can be covered, place 2 tablespoons of fat from broiler. Add onions and sauté for about 2 minutes. Add brown sugar, vinegar, soy sauce, pineapple juice, water, salt, pepper, and ribs. Cover and simmer over low heat for 2 hours. Remove ribs. Thicken sauce with cornstarch mixture. Replace ribs in sauce. (May be frozen at this point, if desired.) When ready to serve, add green pepper, tomato wedges, and pineapple chunks and heat thoroughly. Serve over boiled rice.

SERVES 4-6.

## MARINATED PORK LOIN

2 *pounds pork loin, trimmed*
 MARINADE:
2 *large cloves of garlic, minced*
1 *teaspoon coarse (kosher) salt*
1 *tablespoon thyme*
1 *tablespoon basil*
2 *teaspoons sugar*
 *parsley*
 *cayenne pepper*
1 *tablespoon Dijon mustard*
1 *tablespoon oil*
1 *teaspoon vinegar*

Mix all the marinade ingredients until well blended. Spread over pork loin in a nonaluminum pan. Cover with plastic wrap. Refrigerate 12 hours to 2 days. Return to room temperature before baking. Preheat oven to 325 degrees. Roast until internal temperature measures 150 degrees, approximately 1¼ hours, or 160 degrees for no pinkness. Transfer to cutting board, cover with foil, and let rest 15 minutes before slicing. Deglaze roasting pan with one-half cup water. Bring to boil, thicken with flour and water mixture.

SERVES 4.

This versatile pork dish received rave reviews at the Auxiliary recipe tasting parties.

## NORMANDY PORK CHOPS

6 *pork chops, ¾-inch thick*
½ *teaspoon salt*
 *flour*
 *oil for sautéing*
4 *apples (MacIntosh, Jonathan, or Snow)*
2 *cups fresh cranberries (or 16 ounces canned whole cranberry sauce)*
¾ *cup brown sugar*
1½ *cups cider*

Preheat oven to 325 degrees. Sprinkle pork chops with salt. Dredge with flour. Heat oil in frying pan and sauté chops until golden brown. Pare, core, and thinly slice apples. Lightly oil a 9 x 13-inch glass baking dish. Layer in order cranberries, sugar, apples, and pork chops. Add cider. Cook uncovered 1½ hours. Turn chops halfway through cooking time so both sides are flavored with the fruit sauce. (Note: If using canned cranberry sauce, reduce the brown sugar to taste.)

SERVES 6.

A hearty family-style entrée. Accompany with green beans and a light tossed salad.

## Pork Chops, Onions, and Potatoes

4 medium Idaho potatoes, peeled
4 large loin pork chops
3 tablespoons butter, divided
  salt and pepper
1 medium Bermuda onion (sliced ⅛-inch rings)
1 tablespoon Hungarian paprika
¼ cup water

Slice potatoes into one-eighth-inch rounds. Place in a bowl of cold water and set aside. Brown pork chops in 1 tablespoon of butter in large skillet, 5 minutes on each side. Season with salt and pepper. Remove from skillet and set aside. Preheat oven to 350 degrees. In same skillet, add 2 tablespoons butter and sauté onions until slightly transparent. Add paprika and water. Remove onions to another plate. Deglaze pan with water remaining in pan. Butter a 9 x 13-inch baking dish or similar casserole. Rinse potatoes and drain. Layer potatoes and onions together. Place pork chops on top and pour remaining liquid from skillet over top. Cover with foil and bake at 350 degrees for 35-45 minutes or until potatoes are tender.

SERVES 4.

## Szechwan Pork

1 pound lean pork tenderloin
2 tablespoons vegetable oil
1 large green pepper, cut into ¼-inch strips
1 scallion, sliced
1 teaspoon minced fresh ginger root
1 clove garlic, minced
1 tablespoon black bean sauce
2 tablespoons water
2 tablespoons hoisin sauce
1 tablespoon dry sherry
¼-½ teaspoon chili paste (hot)
1 teaspoon sugar
½ teaspoon salt

Cover pork with water and simmer, covered, for 1 hour, until tender. Cool and slice into ¼-inch slices. Heat oil in wok and stir fry green pepper for 1 minute. Add pork and scallions and continue to stir fry for 1 minute. Combine remaining ingredients and add to pork and green pepper mixture. Heat thoroughly and serve at once with boiled or fried rice. (Note: The black bean sauce, hoisin sauce, and chili paste are available in Oriental grocery shops or gourmet food stores.)

SERVES 2-3.

The tulips are out—yes, out in the cold;

I'm sure they regret that they were so bold

As trying to stand up straight in their bed

While shivering so their lips are all red.

# Poultry
# &
# Game

## FRENCH GARLIC CHICKEN

| | |
|---|---|
| 2 | large heads garlic (20-25 cloves) |
| 1½ | cups chicken stock |
| 2 | tablespoons butter |
| 1 | tablespoon oil |
| 3½-4 | pounds chicken parts |
| 1 | lemon, peeled and thinly sliced |
| 2 | tablespoons flour |
| ½ | cup dry white wine |
| | salt and pepper |

 Preheat oven to 350 degrees. Separate cloves of garlic, set in a saucepan, cover with water, simmer 5 minutes. Drain and cover with cold water. Discard water and peel cloves. Simmer poached, peeled garlic cloves, partially covered, in stock for 30 minutes. In a heavy skillet, melt butter and oil. When hot, brown chicken until golden. Transfer to a 9 x 13-inch pan and cover with garlic cloves and lemon slices. Prepare sauce in skillet with flour, garlic stock, and wine. Skim fat, if necessary, and pour sauce over chicken. Cover with foil and bake for 45-55 minutes. Serve with French bread to spread with poached garlic. May be made ahead and reheated.

SERVES 4-6.

**The French love garlic! Although the number of cloves may appear overwhelming at first, the results are magnifique!**

## COUNTRY CHICKEN AND TOMATOES

| | |
|---|---|
| ⅓ | cup flour |
| 2 | teaspoons black pepper |
| ½ | teaspoon salt |
| ¼ | teaspoon garlic salt |
| 3-4 | pounds frying chicken, cut up |
| ½ | cup butter or margarine |
| 1 | tablespoon diced celery and leaves |
| 1 | tablespoon finely diced green pepper |
| ½ | teaspoon nutmeg |
| ½ | teaspoon dried basil (or 2 teaspoons fresh) |
| 2 | tablespoons finely diced onion |
| 1 | pound fresh mushrooms |
| 1 | cup canned peeled tomatoes, drained and chopped |
| ½ | cup water |

Preheat oven to 350 degrees. Mix together flour, pepper, salt, and garlic salt. Dredge chicken in flour mixture. In a large skillet heat butter or margarine, brown chicken pieces until golden. Transfer chicken to a 9 x 13-inch baking dish. Stir in 1 tablespoon of the seasoned flour mixture to hot skillet; add remaining ingredients. Mix well. Simmer 5 minutes. Pour over chicken and bake uncovered for 45 minutes or until done. Serve over rice.

SERVES 4.

## APRICOT POULET

1  tablespoon margarine or butter, melted
1  tablespoon olive oil
10  skinned chicken breast filets
½  cup white flour
   salt (optional)
   seasoned pepper
¾  cup apricot preserves
¾  cup nonfat yogurt, plain
2  tablespoons Dijon mustard
   slivered almonds

Preheat oven to 375 degrees. Pour melted butter and oil in a shallow baking pan. Mix seasonings with flour in a bag and coat chicken lightly. Place chicken in a single layer in baking pan and bake for 25 minutes. Combine apricot preserves, yogurt, and mustard. Spread apricot mixture on chicken and bake for 30 minutes more. Just before serving, brown almonds lightly and sprinkle over chicken.

SERVES 10.

The creamy apricot-mustard sauce gives the chicken a tangy flavor. Turkey filets can be substituted.

## CRUNCHY KA-BOBS

4  chicken breasts, skinned, boned,
   cut into 1½-inch chunks
¾  cup light Italian salad dressing
1½  cups seasoned bread crumbs
10  ounces canned pineapple chunks
1  medium onion, cut in chunks
½  pound button mushrooms

Dip chicken pieces in Italian dressing and then into seasoned bread crumbs. Alternate chicken pieces with pineapple, onion, and mushrooms on skewers. Barbecue over heated coals or under broiler for 20 minutes or until chicken is done, turning occasionally. Watch carefully to avoid burning crumbs.

SERVES 4.

A welcome change from the traditional shish-ka-bobs. These are especially popular with youngsters.

## Honey Glazed Chicken

¼  cup butter, melted
½  cup honey
¼  cup prepared mustard
1  teaspoon salt
1-2  teaspoons curry powder
3  pounds chicken pieces

Preheat oven to 375 degrees. In a small bowl mix together butter, honey, mustard, salt, and curry powder. Dip chicken pieces in honey mixture and arrange in a single layer in a 3-quart baking dish. Bake for 1 hour or until tender. If using boneless chicken breasts, adjust cooking time according to thickness.

SERVES 3-4.

**A really easy chicken dish which blends beautifully with a side dish of basmatia rice.**

## Chicken Piccata

4  boned and skinless chicken breasts
   salt and pepper
¼  cup flour
4  tablespoons margarine or butter, divided
1½  cups fresh sliced mushrooms
1  garlic clove, minced
¼  cup white wine
2  tablespoons freshly squeezed lemon juice
2  tablespoons chopped parsley

Place chicken between two sheets of waxed paper and pound to a one-half-inch thickness. Salt and pepper breasts and dip in flour. In a large skillet, melt 3 tablespoons of margarine and brown the chicken on both sides. Remove from skillet and keep warm. Add the extra 1 tablespoon of margarine to the skillet and sauté the mushrooms and garlic until tender. Return chicken to pan; add wine and lemon juice. Simmer for 7-10 minutes stirring occasionally, until sauce slightly thickens. Top with chopped parsley.

SERVES 4.

**Here is an elegant entrée which can be completed in 20 minutes.**

## Hawaiian Islands Chicken

½  cup soy sauce
¼  cup bourbon
2  tablespoons brown sugar
¼  teaspoon dry mustard
1  garlic clove, finely minced (or ¼ teaspoon garlic powder)
½  teaspoon ground ginger
8  chicken breasts, boned and skinned
8  fresh pineapple slices

In a mixing bowl, whisk together soy sauce, bourbon, brown sugar, dry mustard, garlic, and ground ginger. Arrange chicken pieces in a single layer in a 9 x 13-inch glass baking dish. Pour marinade over chicken. Cover baking dish and refrigerate for 3-4 hours, turning once or twice while marinating. Grill or broil 5-7 minutes per side, basting several times with marinade. During the last 5 minutes, top each chicken breast with a pineapple slice. Serve immediately.

SERVES 6-8.

**A simple but special way to make chicken on the grill!**

## Chicken Baked with Parmesan

¼  cup olive oil
¼  cup fresh lemon juice
½  teaspoon dried tarragon
⅛  teaspoon ground black pepper
6  chicken breasts, skinned (boning optional)
   garlic salt
6  tablespoons grated Parmesan cheese

In a small bowl, mix together oil, lemon juice, tarragon, and pepper. Pour marinade over chicken, cover and refrigerate 1-2 hours. Preheat oven to 375 degrees. Remove breasts from marinade and arrange close together in an oiled shallow baking dish. Sprinkle lightly with garlic salt and with the Parmesan cheese. Bake for 45 minutes or until tender.

SERVES 6.

## Very Italian Stuffed Chicken Breasts

4   boneless chicken breasts, skinned
⅓   cup ricotta cheese
2   tablespoons grated Parmesan cheese
1   tablespoon sliced green onion
¼   teaspoon dried basil leaves
¼   teaspoon dried oregano leaves
⅛   teaspoon dried thyme leaves
⅛   teaspoon salt
⅛   teaspoon pepper
2   cups of your favorite extra-thick spaghetti
     sauce
1   cup shredded mozzarella cheese

Pound each chicken breast between two sheets of plastic wrap to one-quarter-inch thickness. Set aside. In a small mixing bowl, combine ricotta and Parmesan cheeses, onion, basil, oregano, thyme, salt, and pepper. Mix well. Spread one-quarter of cheese mixture down the center of each chicken breast. Fold in sides and roll up, enclosing filling. Secure with wooden picks. Arrange stuffed rolls seam-side down in a 9-inch square baking dish. Pour spaghetti sauce over chicken. Cover with wax paper. Microwave on high for 15-20 minutes, or until chicken is firm and no longer pink, rotating dish twice. Remove wooden picks. Top with mozzarella cheese. Microwave on medium for 2-4 minutes or until melted. Serve over pasta. (Note: For baking in a conventional oven, cover stuffed breasts with sauce, cheese, then aluminum foil. Bake in a preheated 350 degree oven for 40-50 minutes.)

Serves 4.

## Chicken California Style

4   chicken breasts, boned, skin left on
⅓   fresh orange
½   cup chutney
2   slices white bread, toasted, cubed
¼   cup raisins
2   small celery stalks with leaves, chopped
1   small onion, chopped
½   cup fresh orange juice
½   teaspoon onion powder
½   teaspoon salt
½   teaspoon ground pepper
    Garnish:
1   orange, quartered
4   sprigs parsley

Preheat oven to 350 degrees. Flatten chicken breasts between 2 sheets of waxed paper. In blender, chop together orange and chutney. Toss chutney with toast cubes, raisins, celery, and onion. Place a heaping tablespoon of the mixture in the center of each chicken breast. Fold filet over filling, package-style. Place each stuffed breast in a baking dish, seam-side down. Pour orange juice over top and sprinkle evenly with onion powder, salt, and pepper. Cover dish with foil and bake for 1 hour. Uncover and continue to bake an additional 30 minutes. Garnish the dish with orange wedges and fresh parsley sprigs.

Serves 4.

This chicken entrée, it's said, originated in Pebble Beach. Accompany it with a cracked wheat pilaf and steamed asparagus spears.

## Chicken Fajitas

3   tablespoons canned mild chilies (or 2 Moheim or
    Poblano chili peppers, seeded and cut into
    strips)
2   medium tomatoes, seeded and chopped
1   tablespoon fresh oregano, finely chopped (or 2
    teaspoons dried)
1   teaspoon ground cumin
2   teaspoons chili powder
½   teaspoon salt
2   tablespoons flour
1   pound skinned, boned chicken breasts, cut into
    ½-inch-wide strips
4   tablespoons olive oil, divided
1   large onion, thinly sliced
2   small garlic cloves, finely minced
3   large bell peppers (red, yellow, and green),
    thinly sliced
6   flour tortillas
    GARNISH:
1   cup sour cream
1   cup tomato salsa

Combine chilies, tomatoes, oregano, cumin, chili
powder, salt, and flour with the chicken strips. Mix together well. Set aside. Heat 2 tablespoons of oil in a large
skillet. Sauté onion and garlic until softened, 3-4 minutes.
Add the bell pepper strips and sauté 5 more minutes until
peppers are slightly softened, tender-crisp. Remove from
skillet and keep warm. Heat the second 2 tablespoons of oil
in the skillet. Sauté the chicken strips, stirring and tossing
until chicken is cooked through. Add the sautéed pepper
mixture to the chicken, heat together. Serve the fajita
mixture on warmed tortillas. Garnish each with sour
cream and tomato salsa.

SERVES 4-6.

## Avocados, Apricots, and Chicken

6   large whole chicken breasts, split, boned,
    and skinned
1   teaspoon salt
¼   teaspoon pepper
¼   teaspoon nutmeg
4   tablespoons butter
3   green onions, chopped, including tops
¼   cup dry vermouth
1   cup whipping cream
12  ripe (or canned) apricot halves, pitted
2   tablespoons chopped parsley
1   large avocado, ripe, peeled at serving
1   tablespoon lemon juice

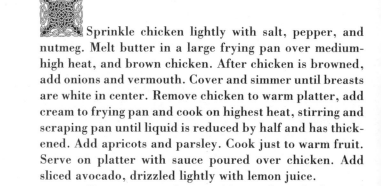

Sprinkle chicken lightly with salt, pepper, and
nutmeg. Melt butter in a large frying pan over medium-
high heat, and brown chicken. After chicken is browned,
add onions and vermouth. Cover and simmer until breasts
are white in center. Remove chicken to warm platter, add
cream to frying pan and cook on highest heat, stirring and
scraping pan until liquid is reduced by half and has thickened. Add apricots and parsley. Cook just to warm fruit.
Serve on platter with sauce poured over chicken. Add
sliced avocado, drizzled lightly with lemon juice.

To prepare in advance: After cooking chicken and
sauce, layer chicken in a casserole dish with the apricots
and parsley on top, then sauce. Heat in 350 degree oven
for 30 minutes or until hot. Arrange avocados on top just
before serving and warm slightly.

SERVES 8-12.

**A colorful dinner entrée
which can be made in
advance.**

## ROASTED HOLIDAY TURKEY

1    *20-pound fresh turkey*
4-6   *tablespoons butter or margarine*
4    *small sage leaves*
14   *cups stuffing (recipe follows)*
4    *tablespoons herbed sherry (see page 185)*

Preheat oven to 325 degrees. Rinse turkey and cavity well. Pat dry. Slip approximately 1 tablespoon of butter and a sage leaf under skin of turkey onto meat on both sides of breast near the wings. Repeat process farther down the breast. Fill cavity with stuffing mix. Do not pack. Overlap skin at opening and secure with trussing skewers. Tie drumsticks together with string or heavy thread. Turn bird over and fill neck loosely with remaining stuffing. Secure skin with skewers. Pull wings back and tuck tips tightly behind shoulders. Place turkey in a shallow rectangular roasting pan breast side up, baste with one-half of the herbed sherry. Cover breast with a large tented sheet of aluminum foil and put in oven. Lift foil and baste bird every hour with pan juices. Rotate pan in oven at least once during roasting time. After 3½ hours, remove foil tent. Baste with remaining herbed sherry. Roast total of 4½-5 hours. Check for doneness (internal temperature 170-175 degrees) using an instant meat thermometer inserted into thickest part of breast and thigh. Juices should run clear when turkey meat is pierced. When bird is done, remove from oven, transfer from roasting pan to a carving board or platter and allow to rest 15 minutes before carving. Prepare gravy while turkey is resting.

STUFFING:

1    *medium onion, chopped*
4    *stalks celery, sliced*
½   *cup plus 2 tablespoons butter, melted*
12   *cups dried, cubed oatmeal bread, corn bread, and herb bread (or favorite commercial herb seasoned stuffing mix)*
½   *pound (1 cup) chestnuts, roasted, peeled, diced*
½   *cup dried cranberries*
½   *cup dried currants*
3-4   *cups chicken stock*

In a medium skillet, sauté onion and celery in 2 tablespoons of melted butter until softened. Remove from heat and set aside. In a large mixing bowl, toss together bread cubes, chestnuts, cranberries, currants, sautéed onion and celery, and remaining melted butter. Add enough stock to soften stuffing.

GRAVY:
*pan drippings*
1-2   *cups turkey or chicken stock*
3    *tablespoons cornstarch dissolved in ⅓ cup cold water*
    *salt and pepper*

Strain drippings from roasting pan into a bowl. Allow fat to rise and remove. Add enough turkey or chicken stock to skimmed drippings to measure 3 cups. Heat in a saucepan. Whisk cornstarch mixture into drippings, simmer about 5 minutes stirring constantly. Season thickened gravy to taste with salt and pepper.

SERVES 14-16.

## CHERRY CORNISH HENS ESCOFFIER

2   tablespoons unsalted butter
2   whole Cornish hens, rinsed, split (or 4 quail)
    salt and pepper
1-2 cups light chicken or veal stock, warmed
½   cup drained, pitted, dark sweet cherries
    (reserve ½ cup juice)
6-8 pieces orange zest, 3 inches long
2   tablespoons black currant or bayberry jam
3   tablespoons kirsch or brandy
    lemon juice as needed
    GARNISH:
8   Belgian endive leaves
4   watercress sprigs

Heat butter in deep skillet. Sauté hens, browning evenly. Season. Add 1 cup warm stock to pan, reduce temperature and simmer covered for 15 minutes, turning once or twice. Add cherries, reserved cherry juice, and orange zest. If liquid seems scanty, add an additional one-half cup of warm stock, continue to simmer 20-25 minutes. Add jam and liqueur. Baste birds and continue to cook until tender, about 15 minutes. Add lemon juice to balance taste. If less than one-quarter cup sauce remains in pan, add up to one-half cup more stock, simmer until sauce is slightly thickened. To serve, pour a small pool of sauce on each plate and place Cornish hen on top. Garnish plate with 2 Belgian endive leaves and a sprig of fresh watercress.

SERVES 4.

## SMOTHERED QUAIL

6   quail (boned)
4   tablespoons butter
1   tablespoon olive oil
1   shallot, sliced into 3-4 pieces
½   cup white wine
½   cup shaved carrots
½   cup chopped celery
½   cup finely chopped onion
    salt and pepper to taste
6   pieces thin toast, crusts trimmed

If quail are frozen, thaw completely. Melt butter in a large skillet and add olive oil. Brown shallot, remove and discard. Brown quail on both sides; add wine, cover, and simmer until quail is tender. Distribute vegetables evenly over quail, cover, and simmer until vegetables are done. Place quail on toast, cover with vegetables, and place in warming oven. Reduce pan drippings by half, over medium-high heat. Season to taste. Pour over quail. Serve immediately.

SERVES 6.

Boning quail is not as tedious as it may appear. The secret is to use a sharp paring knife. Once boned, the meat will cook in a matter of minutes.

## WILD DUCK WITH MUSHROOMS

1    wild duck, quartered
2-3  tablespoons margarine or butter for browning
1    medium onion, sliced
     salt and freshly ground pepper to taste
1    cup duck stock
1    cup beef broth
1    bay leaf
1    cup sliced mushrooms
2    tablespoons margarine or butter for sautéing
2    tablespoons flour
⅛    teaspoon thyme

Brown duck pieces in margarine in casserole. Remove when browned. Add onions and brown. Return duck to casserole. Add salt, pepper, stock, broth, and bay leaf. Cover and simmer 1 hour. Allow to cool in casserole. Chill until fat hardens on top and remove. Bone duck and cut into bite-size pieces. Return to liquid and gently heat. Sauté mushrooms in margarine for 2-3 minutes. Add enough duck liquid to 2 tablespoons of flour to blend smoothly. Add flour mixture and thyme to casserole and continue to heat gently until sauce thickens. Serve over wild rice. To double, use 1 cup of beef broth along with 2 cups of duck stock.

SERVES 2-3.

**An excellent dish to serve during hunting season using fresh or frozen ducks. A good company dish which can be made in advance and easily doubled or tripled.**

## CURRIED DUCK SALAD

2    roasted ducks, about 4 pounds each
1    small onion, finely chopped
2    large ribs celery, finely chopped
2    apples, finely chopped
¼    cup toasted sliced almonds
1    cup mayonnaise
⅔    cup chutney, puréed
8    teaspoons curry powder
2½   teaspoons lemon juice
8    teaspoons honey
1    teaspoon white vinegar
     salt and pepper to taste

When roasted ducks are cooled, bone and dice the meat. Mix with finely chopped onion, celery, and apples along with toasted almonds. In mixing bowl combine mayonnaise, chutney, curry powder, lemon juice, honey, and white vinegar. Blend well. Toss with meat and additional ingredients and season with salt and pepper to taste. Chill and let marinate at least 2 hours before serving.

SERVES 8.

**The Lark Restaurant
West Bloomfield, Michigan**

## Roast Pheasant

3 pheasants
3 tablespoons bacon fat
1 onion, small, chopped
1 apple, small, chopped
½ cup dry Madeira
⅔ cup game or veal stock
  salt
1 teaspoon thyme leaves
6 bay leaves
20 peppercorns
6 juniper berries
6 allspice berries
1 tablespoon arrowroot
1 heaping tablespoon cold butter

Preheat oven to 300 degrees. Cut off legs and wings from breasts; split legs through backbone. Remove wishbones from breasts to facilitate carving, set breasts aside. In a sautoir or deep skillet, sear legs and wings in bacon fat on both sides, remove; drain excess fat if necessary, add onion and apple, sauté until tender. Deglaze pan with wine and half of the stock. Season legs and wings with salt, place back in sautoir, add seasonings; bring to simmer on top of stove, cover and place in 300 degree oven. Cook legs for approximately 1½ hours, or until tender; transfer to another dish, keep warm. Strain pan juice to a small saucepan; discard wings and vegetable-spice residue; skim fat if excessive. Dissolve arrowroot in the rest of the stock, pour into juice, bring to boil, taste and correct seasonings. Remove sauce from fire, whisk in butter; keep warm.

**For Roasting Breasts:**
  salt, pepper, thyme
3 sheets thin-sliced back fat, about 5 x 6 inches
  string for tying
2 tablespoons clarified butter

To roast breasts (35 minutes before serving time): Preheat oven to 450 degrees. Season breasts with salt, pepper, and thyme; cover each with a sheet of fat, tie on with a string. Preheat a suitable skillet or roasting pan; pour in clarified butter, place breasts in and sear on all sides. Transfer pan to preheated oven; roast exactly 25 minutes. During this time, pull tendons out of drumsticks, remove pelvic bone from legs; reheat legs in sauce, gently, without boiling. Remove breasts from oven, allow to rest for a few minutes; drain fat from roast pan, deglaze with sauce. Remove string and fat from breasts; carve, slicing parallel to breastbone. To serve, place a leg on a plate, fan breast slices over one side of leg. Spoon sauce over.

SERVES 6.

**The Golden Mushroom**
**Southfield, Michigan**

**Young pheasants may be roasted whole; however, the legs of a mature bird will become tough and are best when braised.**

## Venison Loin with Cherry Sauce

Demi-Glace:

*(To be prepared a day in advance)*

3  *pounds venison shanks*
3  *pounds veal shanks*
1  *onion, cut into large cubes*
2  *carrots, peeled, cut into large cubes*
3  *celery ribs, peeled, cut into large cubes*
1  *tomato, peeled, seeded, cut into large cubes*
1  *bay leaf*
3  *sprigs thyme*
   *cornstarch (optional)*
   *red wine (optional)*

Preheat oven to 400 degrees. Roast veal and venison shanks with onions, carrots, celery, and tomato until dark brown. Place bones, vegetables, bay leaf, and thyme in a stock pot, add enough cold water just to cover. Slowly bring to a boil, skim the surface, then reduce heat to a low simmer. Cook for 12 hours being careful to skim off residue and fat periodically. Strain liquid through a colander lined with cheesecloth. Return stock back to a clean stock pot. Bring to a boil and reduce by three-quarters. Adjust consistency with a mixture of cornstarch and red wine if necessary, season to taste. Refrigerate.

Venison Loin with Cherry Sauce:

2  *pounds venison loin, trimmed*
2  *ounces whole black peppercorns*
1  *ounce whole juniper berries*
2  *ounces clarified butter*
   *salt to taste*
1  *cup red wine*
⅓  *cup sun-dried cherries*

Cut venison into 8 medallions. Grind the black pepper and juniper berries. Dredge the venison in ground pepper-berry mixture, shake off excess. Heat clarified butter in skillet and sauté meat about 2 minutes on the first side, turn meat and sear other side, reduce heat to low. Season and remove from pan when cooked rare. Remove to drain on paper toweling and keep warm. Deglaze skillet with red wine, add cherries, and reduce liquid. Add demi-glace and reduce to a medium-thick consistency. Spoon sauce onto each plate and set sautéed venison medallions on top.

Serves 4.

Meadowbrook Hall
Rochester, Michigan

This recipe was submitted in 1990 to the School for American Chefs, Beringer Vineyards, California, by scholarship winner Chef Steven Machlay along with Autumn Leaves (see Vegetables) and Poached Pears with Blackberry Wine Sorbet (see Breakfast and Brunch).

The crocuses are croaking on the lawn

But bullfrogs croak much louder—

Especially long before the crack of dawn

And clams swim in the chowder.

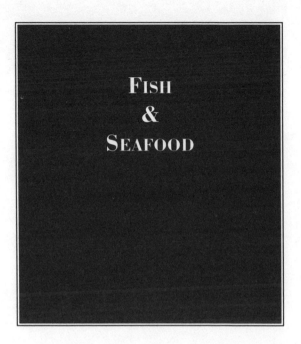

# FISH
# &
# SEAFOOD

## Salmon and Lake Trout Medallions with Sauces "Deux Champagnes"

1   medium Norwegian salmon filet, skinned and
    boned
1   medium lake trout filet, skinned and boned
2   tablespoons unsalted butter, diced
1   cup fish stock
2   tablespoons freshly chopped parsley

Preheat oven to 325 degrees. Cut each fish filet into 4-6 pieces. Take each piece of salmon and match with a piece of trout and invert them together having the "skin" side out. Using two toothpicks, fasten the fish filets together to form a "medallion." Repeat with all fish pieces. Lightly butter a fish poacher or glass baking dish. Place the fish medallions in, cover with the fish stock, parsley, and the rest of the 2 tablespoons of butter, and cover. Heat on the stove to a gentle boil, then place in oven for 8-10 minutes or until fish is medium-rare. With a slotted spatula, remove medallions to serving plates, gently remove all the toothpicks and keep warm while making the sauces. Reserve the cooking liquid.

Sauces "Deux Champagnes":
½   bottle of "Blanc de Blancs" sparkling wine
½   bottle of "Blanc de Noir" sparkling wine
1   cup fish stock or clam juice
1   cup dry white wine
    juice and zest of two lemons
1   tablespoon chopped fresh herbs (your choice)
2   tablespoons chopped shallots
½   pound unsalted butter, chilled and diced
    salt and fresh ground pepper to taste
Garnish:
1   lemon (seeds removed), thinly sliced
    bouquets of fresh herbs

Place the "Blanc de Blancs" in one sauté pan and the "Blanc de Noir" in the other. Divide the fish stock, white wine, lemon juice and zest, chopped herbs, chopped shallots, and one-half cup of the reserved cooking liquid between the two pans. On medium-high heat, cook the contents of both pans until the liquids are reduced by half. Quickly whisk in half the chilled butter into each pan over medium heat, a piece at a time, until the sauces form. Season to taste with salt and pepper. Pass each sauce through a fine mesh strainer over its particular side of each medallion: the "blond" sauce over the salmon, and the "pink" sauce over the trout. Quickly garnish with lemon slices and bouquets of herbs; serve immediately.

Serves 4-6.

Van Dyke Place
Detroit, Michigan

An elegant company entrée
worthy of discerning palates.

## SPANISH NATIONAL "PAELLA"

3 pounds chicken cut into small pieces
 olive oil as needed
½ cup chopped onions
¼ cup diced green peppers
¼ cup diced red peppers
1 tablespoon chopped garlic
½ cup sliced Chorizo sausage
2 cups rice
¾ cup peeled and diced tomatoes
¼ cup green pitted olives
¼ cup black pitted olives
1 cup clam juice
1 cup garbanzos, cooked and drained
⅓ teaspoon saffron
4 cups concentrated chicken stock
 salt and pepper to taste
1 pound large shrimp, peeled and deveined
8 little necks, cleaned
8 mussels, cleaned

In a large paella pan or heavy ovenproof skillet, sauté chicken in olive oil. Remove chicken and set aside. Sauté onions, peppers, and garlic. Add sausage and rice. Mix well. Add tomatoes, olives, clam juice, garbanzos, and chicken. Add saffron to chicken stock, adjust seasonings with salt and pepper. Bring stock to a boil and pour into pan. Cover and cook for 10 minutes.

Preheat oven to 375 degrees. Add shrimp, clams, and mussels to pan. Cover and cook in oven for 10 minutes. Paella should retain some moisture. The rice should be reasonably firm, not dried out.

SERVES 8.

**Machus Red Fox Restaurant**
**Birmingham, Michigan**

Paella ingredients usually relate to product availability in a specific area. Any reasonable additions and substitutions can be made... also very expensive ones, such as lobster tails and scampi, etc.

## CRACKIN' CAJUN SHRIMP

½ pound butter, melted
½ pound margarine, melted
⅜-½ cup Worcestershire sauce
4 tablespoons black pepper
1 teaspoon ground rosemary
2 teaspoons Tabasco sauce
2 lemons, juice only
2 teaspoons salt (sea salt)
3 cloves garlic, minced
5-6 pounds large shrimp in their shells
2 lemons, sliced thin

Preheat oven to 400 degrees. In a bowl, mix melted butter, margarine, Worcestershire, pepper, rosemary, Tabasco, lemon juice, salt, and garlic. Pour about a half cup of sauce to cover the bottom of a large baking dish; arrange layers of shrimp and lemon slices until almost to the top of the dish. Leave about 1 inch of headroom. Pour the remaining sauce over the shrimp and lemon slices. Bake, uncovered, stirring once or twice until the shrimp are cooked through, about 15-20 minutes. Serve with hot French bread, generous napkins, and a bowl for the shrimp shells. Open the shrimp shells with your fingers and dip the bread into the sauce.

SERVES 8-10.

A "finger licking" entrée for casual entertaining.

## SHRIMP FLAMBÉ

¼ small lemon
2 stalks celery, bias sliced into 1-inch pieces
3 green onions, sliced into 1-inch lengths
1 clove garlic, minced
3 tablespoons butter or margarine
¾ pound large shelled shrimp
1 cup canned tomatoes, cut up
¼ teaspoon dried basil, crushed
¼ teaspoon salt
freshly ground pepper
dash bottled hot pepper sauce
¼ cup slivered almonds, toasted
¼ cup Southern Comfort or brandy
2 cups hot cooked rice

With zester or sharp knife, cut lemon peel into thin strips. Set aside. In a skillet, sauté celery, onion, and garlic in butter until tender; do not brown. Add shrimp. Continue cooking 2-3 minutes or until shrimp are pink and curled. Add undrained tomatoes, basil, salt, pepper, and hot pepper sauce. Stir over low heat for 2-3 minutes. When hot, stir in almonds. In a small saucepan, heat Southern Comfort or brandy and lemon peel just until warm. Arrange shrimp over rice on a platter. Ignite warmed brandy. Pour over shrimp mixture. Allow flames to subside before serving.

SERVES 4.

## SHRIMP BAYOU

⅔  cup oil
½  cup flour
⅔  cup chopped green pepper
⅔  cup chopped celery
 1  cup chopped onions
½  cup chopped shallots
 1  tablespoon minced garlic
10  medium tomatoes, skinned, chopped, and
    drained (or 3 cups canned tomatoes, chopped
    and drained)
⅔  cup water
 2  teaspoons lemon juice
 1  teaspoon dried parsley
 2  bay leaves
½  teaspoon chili powder
½  teaspoon creole seasoning
 5  whole allspice berries
½  teaspoon dried basil leaves
½  teaspoon dried thyme
 1  tablespoon freshly ground pepper
½  teaspoon ground cayenne pepper
    salt to taste
 2  pounds fresh shrimp, peeled and deveined

In a heavy 8-quart stock pot, heat oil. Gradually add flour and stir constantly over low heat until a dark brown roux is formed. Add chopped pepper, celery, onions, shallots, and garlic; stir until vegetables begin to brown. Stir in tomatoes, water, lemon juice, and all the seasonings. Increase heat and bring mixture to a boil. Lower heat and simmer for 45 minutes until mixture is thick. Add shrimp. Bring to boil, cover pot and simmer for 10 minutes until the shrimp are tender. Serve immediately. Accompany with white rice.

SERVES 6-8.

A regional classic made with a new twist! Complement the spicy Creole flavor with a light tossed green salad and hot corn bread for a festive meal.

## Shrimp New York, New York

1 pound fresh large shelled shrimp
2 tablespoons butter
1 egg
¼ cup heavy cream
¼ cup feta cheese, crumbled
4-6 dashes Tabasco sauce
1 large tomato, peeled and sliced
½ lemon
1 tablespoon chopped parsley
freshly ground pepper

Preheat oven to 350 degrees. In a medium skillet, sauté shrimp in butter until barely cooked. Remove shrimp and arrange in a single layer in baking dish. Combine egg and cream, add cheese and Tabasco, and pour over shrimp. Arrange tomato slices on top. Bake until bubbly hot, 25-30 minutes. Squeeze lemon evenly over top, sprinkle with chopped parsley and freshly ground pepper.

SERVES 4.

A delicious and easy make-ahead company entrée. Can be prepared early in the day, refrigerated, then baked before serving. Good with seasoned rice or orzo.

## Shrimp de Jonghe

½ cup butter or margarine, melted
2 cloves garlic, minced
⅓ cup parsley, finely chopped
½ teaspoon paprika
¼ teaspoon cayenne pepper
½ cup dry white wine
2 cups seasoned bread crumbs
4 cups cooked shrimp, peeled, deveined
GARNISH:
6 tablespoons chopped parsley or mixed fresh herbs

Preheat oven to 350 degrees. In a medium bowl, stir together melted butter, garlic, parsley, paprika, cayenne, and wine. Stir in bread crumbs. Place shrimp in 12 x 7½ x 2-inch baking dish. Spread butter mixture over top. Bake 25 minutes or until crumbs are brown. Garnish with chopped parsley or herbs.

SERVES 6 (OR 8 AS APPETIZER).

Smaller portions of this dish make a tasty appetizer.

## MICROWAVE SALMON WITH FRESH DILL

1   pound fresh salmon filets
⅓   cup mayonnaise
¼   teaspoon garlic salt
1   tablespoon fresh chopped dill
2   medium fresh tomatoes, quartered and seeded
    GARNISH:
    sprigs of dill or parsley

Place fish in large oval microwave casserole. Do not overlap. Spread with mayonnaise and sprinkle with garlic salt and dill. Cover with plastic wrap and cook on high 3 minutes. Turn filets and arrange tomato quarters around fish. Cover and continue cooking 3 additional minutes. Garnish with dill or parsley sprigs.

SERVES 3-4.

## MARYLAND CRAB CAKES

1   pound lump crabmeat (preferably Maryland)
1-2 tablespoons all-purpose flour
1   egg
¼   cup heavy cream
⅛   teaspoon salt
¼   teaspoon pepper
⅛   teaspoon red cayenne pepper
¼   cup butter or margarine

Rinse and strain crabmeat, being careful to remove shells. In a medium bowl, toss 1 tablespoon flour and crabmeat together gently. Beat egg, cream, and seasonings together. Pour over crabmeat, adding enough flour to allow shaping into cakes, and toss lightly. In heavy skillet, melt butter. Using a large tablespoon, shape crabmeat slightly and drop into hot butter. Turn once when golden brown. They cook very quickly.

SERVES 4.

These are especially delicious when served with roasted herb potatoes and garlic bread.

## MARVELS OF THE SEA

¾   cup butter, divided
4   tablespoons flour
1   pint half & half, heated
⅛   teaspoon ground mace
¼   teaspoon salt
¼   teaspoon Tabasco sauce
⅛   teaspoon white pepper
4   tablespoons dry white wine
14  ounces canned artichoke hearts
½   pound fresh button mushrooms, cleaned and
    trimmed
½   pound fresh lump crab meat or frozen Alaskan
    king crab, thawed and drained
½   pound cooked, peeled, and deveined shrimp

Preheat oven to 325 degrees. Melt one-half cup
butter in top of double boiler over rapidly boiling water.
Blend in flour. Slowly stir in hot half & half. Add mace,
salt, Tabasco, and pepper. Cook and stir until sauce is
smooth and thickened. Taste and correct seasonings. Add
white wine after sauce has thickened. Rinse artichoke
hearts in cold water, drain, and dry on paper towel. Trim
and cut each in half. Sauté mushrooms in 4 tablespoons
butter, add artichoke hearts stirring until warm. Pour
into a large (9 x 13-inch) buttered casserole dish. Add
crabmeat and shrimp. Cover with white sauce. Cover with
foil and bake for 20-30 minutes, or until sauce is bubbly.
Be careful not to overcook!

SERVES 8.

**Reheats well, but not recom-
mended for freezing.**

## PESCE LESSO

1   clove garlic, minced
1   leek, diced (white part only)
1   carrot, diced
3   large mushrooms, sliced
3   tablespoons olive oil
1½  pounds fish filets (flounder, snapper, pike, sole)
½   teaspoon dried basil
½   teaspoon dried marjoram
    pinch dried thyme
    pinch ground allspice
2   tablespoons chopped parsley
    salt and pepper
2   tablespoons dry Madeira or dry Marsala wine
½   cup clam juice
    GARNISH:
5-6 lemon wedges
    sprigs of parsley or fresh herbs

Preheat oven to 450 degrees. Lightly brown
chopped garlic, leeks, carrot, and mushrooms in olive oil.
Spread evenly on bottom of an oiled 9 x 13-inch glass or
ceramic baking dish. Arrange fish filets over vegetables.
Season with herbs, salt and pepper, add wine and clam
juice. Cover fish with a sheet of aluminium foil or parchment paper lightly brushed with oil, tucking paper into
dish. Bake for 10-14 minutes. When tender, remove filets
to a serving plate. Strain juices and pour over fish. Garnish with lemon wedges and mini bouquets of parsley or
fresh herbs.

SERVES 4.

**A specialty of northern Italy
which can be prepared in 30
minutes or less.**

## PROVENÇAL FISH STEW

2   tablespoons extra-virgin olive oil
1   medium leek, sliced (white part only)
1   medium onion, peeled, sliced
2   large garlic cloves, finely minced
2   medium carrots, peeled, sliced
2   medium tomatoes, peeled, quartered
1   quart vegetable or fish stock
1½  pounds mixed fish filets, at least 3 varieties such
    as scrod, sole, and catfish
12  shrimp, shelled, deveined
12  mussels in the shell, scrubbed
1   tablespoon pesto or finely chopped basil
    pinch dried oregano
    salt
    freshly ground pepper

Heat olive oil in a large heavy saucepan. Add sliced leek, onion, and garlic, sautéing over medium heat until onion and leek are softened. Add sliced carrots, tomato, and stock. Bring to a boil, simmer until carrots are tender. Cut fish fillets into 2 x 2-inch pieces. Add fish, shrimp, and mussels to simmering soup. Reduce to low heat and allow fish to cook gently for 10 minutes. Add pesto or basil and oregano. Adjust seasonings with salt and pepper. Serve with thick slices of crunchy French bread.

SERVES 4.

**A hearty stew similar to bouillabaisse, flavored with basil instead of saffron.**

## NEW ENGLAND SCALLOP CHOWDER

2   tablespoons butter or margarine
2   medium leeks, sliced, white part only
2   large garlic cloves, finely minced
2   medium potatoes, peeled, diced
2½  cups warm vegetable broth or bouillon
¾   pound sea or bay scallops, rinsed, sliced
¾   cup cooked corn kernels
¼   teaspoon dried thyme
    salt and pepper
½   tablespoon potato starch mixed in 2 tablespoons
    cold water for thickening

In a heavy saucepan, heat butter. Add minced leeks and garlic. Sauté over medium heat until softened, add potatoes and stock. Continue cooking until potatoes are soft and falling apart. Remove from heat and purée. Return to saucepan, add sliced scallops, corn, and thyme. Heat until scallops are cooked, 5-10 minutes. Add salt and pepper to taste. To thicken chowder, pour potato starch mixture into hot chowder stirring constantly. Adjust seasonings. Bring soup to a quick boil and remove from heat.

SERVES 4.

**Sea and bay scallops are interchangeable in this recipe, but often bay scallops are preferred because of their sweet flavor.**

## Seafood Fettucine

## Orange Roughy with Kiwi

2   tablespoons butter
2   garlic cloves, minced
½   cup sliced scallions
1   pint fresh mushrooms, sliced
¾   pound (24) shrimp, peeled and deveined
¾   pound sea scallops
¼   cup white wine
1   bunch or 2 large stalks broccoli, cut into florets
1   small head cauliflower, trimmed, cut into chunks
24  fresh Chinese pea pods
3   medium carrots, sliced diagonally
12  ounces multi-colored fettucine noodles
1   cup sour cream (or low-fat plain yogurt)
½   cup grated Parmesan cheese
     lemon pepper to taste
     seasoned salt to taste
     salt and pepper to taste

Melt butter in a large skillet. When hot, sauté garlic, scallions, and mushrooms. When mushrooms are tender, remove and set aside, then add shrimp and scallops. Cook, stirring over medium high heat about 6 minutes. After milk runs from scallops and the shrimp curl, add white wine. Simmer 1 minute. Remove from heat and set aside. In boiling water, blanch broccoli, cauliflower, pea pods, and carrots approximately 5 minutes. Drain and set aside. Boil pasta until tender; drain. Butter a 9 x 13-inch baking dish. Add shrimp, scallops, mushrooms, vegetables, and pasta. Blend sour cream, Parmesan cheese, lemon pepper, seasoned salt, salt and pepper; pour over above mixture and toss. Reheat quickly in a microwave or in a moderate oven for 10 minutes or until hot.

SERVES 4-6.

4   frozen orange roughy fish filets (about ½ pound each), thawed
½   cup dry white wine
3   tablespoons fresh lemon juice
     salt and pepper
4   tablespoons finely chopped parsley
2   whole kiwi fruit, peeled and sliced
     GARNISH:
2   whole red peppers, sliced in rings
     paprika
4   lemon wedges

Preheat oven to 425 degrees. Place fish filets in a 13 x 9-inch baking dish. Pour wine in bottom of dish, sprinkle filets with lemon juice, salt and pepper, and chopped parsley. Top with kiwi slices. Lightly grease a sheet of parchment paper and tuck into baking dish or cover with aluminum foil. Bake for 15 minutes. Test for doneness with a fork. (Note: This dish may also be cooked in a microwave oven.) To serve, arrange 3 red pepper rings on individual plates, top with a cooked filet, sprinkle with paprika, and garnish with a lemon wedge.

SERVES 4.

**Any favorite seasonal white fish filet could be substituted.**

Seeds are in tomato,

Sugar's in my cake;

In my mashed potato

There's a yellow lake.

# Vegetables
## Pasta
## &
## Rice

## Sautéed Broccoli Rape with Fresh Fava Beans

2  pounds unshelled young fava beans
3  tablespoons olive oil
2  cloves garlic, slivered
⅛  pound pancetta (Italian bacon), cut into ¼-inch-wide strips
1  large bunch broccoli rape, washed, torn, and trimmed of tough stems
   salt and freshly ground pepper

 Shell the fava beans and blanch in rapidly boiling salted water for 30 seconds. Rinse in cold water and, using your fingers, slip the beans from their outer skins. In a large skillet, heat the olive oil and sauté the garlic slowly being careful not to brown it. Add the pancetta and sauté until it has rendered its fat. Add the fava beans and sauté until they begin to soften, about 5 minutes. Add the broccoli rape and sauté over a medium flame, stirring occasionally, until tender. Season to taste with salt and pepper and serve.

SERVES 4.

**Martha Stewart**
**Food and Entertainment Author**

## Tortilla Medley

1  large Spanish onion
2  green peppers
2  yellow peppers
2  red peppers
¼  cup olive oil
2  cloves garlic
12  (7-inch) flour tortillas
4  cups shredded medium-sharp Cheddar cheese
8  ounces sour cream (or plain yogurt)
8  ounces hot salsa

 Peel and slice onion into strips. Seed and slice peppers into strips. Heat olive oil in large skillet over medium high heat. Peel garlic and swirl into hot oil. Add peppers and onion and sauté until crisp tender (5-10 minutes). Discard garlic cloves. Set skillet aside and keep warm. Warm tortillas in a 350 degree oven for about one minute. Sprinkle one-third cup cheese on each tortilla and allow to melt. Remove from oven. Spoon onion-pepper mixture down center of each cheese-topped tortilla, and fold over sides. Serve sour cream or yogurt and salsa on the side.

SERVES 6.

Colorful and zesty, this Spanish vegetable dish is an ideal entrée for a meatless meal.

## ARTICHOKE HEARTS SURPRISE

2  tablespoons butter or margarine
1  onion, diced
20  ounces frozen artichoke hearts, thawed
1  tablespoon lemon juice
½  teaspoon salt or to taste
½  teaspoon pepper
½  pound fresh broccoli florets (or 10 ounces
    frozen chopped broccoli)
2  chicken bouillon cubes dissolved in hot water
1  cup cream sauce made with 2 tablespoons flour,
    2 tablespoons butter, ¾ cup evaporated milk,
    salt and pepper
2  tablespoons Parmesan cheese

Preheat oven to 375 degrees. Butter a 1-quart baking dish and set aside. In a skillet heat butter, add onion and artichoke hearts. Sauté until onion is softened. Season with lemon juice, salt and pepper. Transfer to baking dish and arrange hearts evenly. Cook broccoli in chicken bouillon until very tender. Drain. Mash with potato masher. Set aside. To prepare cream sauce, melt butter in a saucepan, stir in flour; when evenly mixed, slowly add evaporated milk. Cook until thickened, remove from heat and stir in cheese. Add seasonings. Mix with broccoli and spread over artichoke hearts. Bake for 10 minutes until hot.

SERVES 6-8.

## SPINACH-ARTICHOKE-OYSTER COMBO

40  ounces frozen chopped spinach (or 2½ pounds
    fresh)
20  ounces frozen artichoke hearts
1  quart fresh oysters
8  tablespoons butter or margarine
1  medium onion, diced
1  bunch green onions, diced
1  green pepper, cored and diced
   juice of 1 large lemon
8  ounces cream cheese, softened
⅓  cup Italian bread crumbs, divided

Preheat oven to 350 degrees. Cook spinach and artichoke hearts according to package directions. Drain well. In a saucepan, cook oysters in liquid until edges curl, remove from heat. Drain. Heat butter in a large skillet. Sauté onion, green onions, and green pepper until golden. Add spinach and juice of lemon. Add cream cheese and stir until smooth. Add enough bread crumbs to absorb butter. In a buttered 3-quart casserole or soufflé dish, arrange artichoke hearts on bottom of dish. Add oysters, then place spinach mixture on top of oysters. Dot with butter, sprinkle remaining bread crumbs and a few more drops of lemon juice. Heat in moderate oven. May be made in advance, refrigerated, and reheated for 30 minutes at 350 degrees.

SERVES 10.

## Autumn Leaves

28 individual green beans of equal length
28 individual yellow wax beans of equal length
1 red pepper
8 whole fresh or dried morels
2 tablespoons butter
1 shallot, minced
5 fresh sprigs thyme leaves, minced
   salt and pepper to taste

 Remove ends from green and yellow beans. Blanch in boiling, salted water for 2 minutes. Drain and set beans in ice water. Roast red pepper over open flame until blackened. Peel, then slice in half removing core and seeds. When cool, slice into strips, 2½ x ¼ inch. Set aside. If using dry morels, rehydrate in a minimal amount of hot water for 4 minutes. Remove and drain on paper towelling. Clean fresh morels by hand, rinse, then slice in half lengthwise. Melt butter in skillet or sauté pan. When hot, add minced shallot and thyme. When butter turns hazelnut in color, add all the vegetables, reduce heat to low and simmer until tender. Season with salt and pepper to taste.

SERVES 4.

**Meadowbrook Hall
Rochester, Michigan**

**An attractive mixture
of fresh vegetables and
Michigan morels.**

## Broccoli Bake

1 large head broccoli, cut in spears
16 ounces canned plum tomatoes
2 tablespoons butter
2 tablespoons flour
½ cup sour cream
¼ teaspoon garlic powder
½ teaspoon fresh lemon juice
½ cup grated sharp Cheddar cheese

 Cook broccoli spears in boiling water until almost tender. Drain. Remove and set in a greased 2-quart casserole or baking dish. Drain tomatoes, reserving liquid. Arrange tomatoes over broccoli and set aside. Preheat oven to 350 degrees. In a medium skillet melt butter, add flour, stirring over low heat until blended. Add sour cream, garlic powder, tomato liquid, lemon juice, and then cheese, stirring constantly until well blended. Pour sauce over vegetables. Bake uncovered 10-15 minutes.

SERVES 4-5.

## RED CABBAGE TO BLUE KRAUT

1   head red cabbage, 2-3 pounds
3   tablespoons butter
2   tablespoons sugar
1   large apple, peeled, cored, and chopped
1   medium onion, chopped
¼   cup white or wine vinegar
1-2   cups water or chicken stock, as needed
⅓   cup red currant jelly (or other tart jelly)
     salt to taste

Trim cabbage, quarter, rinse, drain, and shred, discarding core and tough ribs. Heat butter in a large Dutch oven or casserole. Add sugar and sauté slowly until golden brown. Add apple and onion, cover and braise over low heat 3-4 minutes. Add the shredded cabbage and toss until it is coated with fat. Pour vinegar over the cabbage and stir to mix thoroughly. Cover pot and braise slowly about 10 minutes or until cabbage has turned "blue" (bright purple). Add 1 cup water or broth. Cover and simmer slowly 1½-2 hours, or until cabbage is tender. Add more liquid if needed as cabbage cooks. Add currant jelly, stirring until melted. Season with salt.

SERVES 6.

The key to making blue kraut is braising the cabbage in hot fat and vinegar before adding the liquid. The flavor of this popular buffet dish is best when made a day or so in advance.

## CARROTS WITH LEMON AND DILL

1   pound carrots cut into ½-inch pieces
2   tablespoons butter
½   cup minced onion
¼   cup dry white wine
½   teaspoon grated lemon zest
2   tablespoons fresh lemon juice
2   tablespoons minced fresh dill
     salt and white pepper to taste

Steam carrots for 7-8 minutes or until tender-crisp. In a skillet, heat butter and sauté onion until softened. Add carrots, wine, lemon zest, and one tablespoon of the lemon juice. Cook, stirring until most of the liquid is reduced, about 2 minutes. Add the dill, salt and white pepper, and additional lemon juice to taste. Serve hot.

SERVES 4.

## Cauliflower Medley

1   *large head cauliflower, trimmed into florets*
8   *tablespoons butter or margarine, divided*
½   *cup chopped celery*
½   *cup chopped green pepper*
½   *cup chopped onion*
4   *tablespoons flour*
2   *cups milk*
1   *cup shredded extra-sharp Cheddar cheese*
3   *large fresh tomatoes, sliced*
2   *cups fresh bread crumbs*

Preheat oven to 350 degrees. Bring a large pot of water to a boil. Add cauliflower and simmer 5 minutes. Drain, rinse under cold water and drain again. Melt 6 tablespoons butter in a large skillet and add celery, green pepper, and onion. Sauté 5 minutes. Stir flour into vegetable mixture until blended. Add milk, stirring until mixture thickens. Add cheese, stirring until melted. In a 9 x 13-inch baking dish, put a layer of cauliflower, pour on one-third of the sauce, top with a layer of sliced tomatoes. Repeat twice more, forming three layers. Melt remaining 2 tablespoons butter and mix with bread crumbs; sprinkle on top. Bake 20-30 minutes.

Serves 8.

## Cucumbers and Cream

3   *cucumbers, peeled, trimmed*
2   *bunches red radishes (12-16), trimmed*
12   *scallions, trimmed (white part only)*
½   *cup sour cream*
1   *tablespoon lemon juice*
1   *tablespoon vinegar*
½   *teaspoon salt*
½   *tablespoon sugar*
    *dash freshly ground pepper*

Slice the cucumbers, radishes, and scallions very thinly. Beat together the sour cream, lemon juice, vinegar, and seasonings. Combine sour cream mixture with the vegetables and refrigerate 2-3 hours before serving.

Serves 4.

## SWEET AND SOUR MUSHROOMS AND CABBAGE

6   slices bacon
2   tablespoons butter
½   cup minced onion
1   pound mushrooms, sliced
4   cups slivered cabbage
¼   cup water
2   tablespoons vinegar
1   tablespoon brown sugar
1   teaspoon dill seed
¼   teaspoon pepper

In a large skillet sauté bacon until crisp; remove, crumble, and set aside. Drain all but 2 tablespoons fat from pan, add butter and melt. Sauté onions and mushrooms for 5 minutes. Add remaining ingredients including bacon. Bring to boiling point, reduce heat, cover and simmer for 7 minutes or until cabbage is crisp-tender.

SERVES 8.

**Although there are many varieties of cabbage available throughout the year, the new or green cabbage is best for braising. A pungent accompaniment to grilled chicken, sausages, or lamb.**

## SWEET ONION PUDDING

½   cup butter
2   cups chopped sweet onions, such as Vidalia
    or Walla Walla
¼   cup flour
    salt and pepper to taste
12  ounces evaporated milk
2   large eggs, beaten

Preheat oven to 425 degrees. In medium skillet, heat butter and sauté onions until golden. Blend in flour and seasoning. Add milk, stirring constantly. Remove from heat; cool 5 minutes. Slowly add beaten eggs while stirring. Pour into a 10-inch round baking dish. Bake 30-45 minutes or until well set. Can be made ahead, refrigerated, and then baked.

SERVES 4-6.

**A versatile side dish which is well received during the winter doldrums.**

## GEORGIAN SWEET POTATO SOUFFLÉ

3  large sweet potatoes
2  large eggs
½  cup milk
¼  cup sugar
½  teaspoon orange juice concentrate
½  teaspoon fresh grated nutmeg

 In a medium saucepan, boil sweet potatoes in their jackets until tender (20 minutes). Remove, cool, and peel. Preheat oven to 350 degrees. In a blender, mix eggs, milk, sugar, juice, and nutmeg until blended. Add potatoes and purée. Spoon into a 2-quart buttered soufflé or casserole dish and bake for 30-40 minutes.

SERVES 4-6.

This puffy potato dish is delectable enough to be served as a dessert.

## ROASTED ROSEMARY POTATO SLICES

5  tablespoons unsalted butter, melted
4  russet (baking) potatoes (about 1¼ pounds),
   scrubbed
1  teaspoon coarse (kosher) salt
1  teaspoon crumbled dried rosemary
   (or 2 teaspoons finely chopped fresh)
   freshly ground pepper to taste

 Preheat oven to 425 degrees. Pour half the butter into an 8-inch baking pan, making sure it covers the entire bottom. Cut the potatoes into one-quarter-inch-thick slices. In the pan, layer the potatoes in separate rows, overlapping the slices slightly. Sprinkle with salt, rosemary, and pepper. Drizzle the remaining butter over the potatoes. Bake in the middle of the oven, turning each row once with a long thin spatula, for 45 minutes to 1 hour, or until they are crisp and golden.

SERVES 4.

Delicately aromatic, this side dish from Provence, France is ideal with almost any entrée, but especially lamb, chicken, or salmon.

## PUFFED POTATO PIE

1 (10-inch) unbaked pastry pie shell
1 pound cottage cheese
2 cups mashed potatoes
½ cup sour cream
2 eggs
⅛ teaspoon salt
⅛ teaspoon cayenne
½ cup scallions, sliced (white part only)
3 tablespoons grated Parmesan cheese

 Preheat oven to 425 degrees. Put cottage cheese through a food mill to make it smooth. Beat the mashed potatoes into the cottage cheese. Beat in the sour cream, eggs, salt, and cayenne. Stir in scallions. Spoon into unbaked pastry shell. Sprinkle with grated cheese. Bake for 50 minutes or until golden brown.

SERVES 8.

**A refreshing change from traditional quiche. One slice is rich enough to be served as a luncheon or dinner entrée.**

## BAKED FRESH TOMATOES

8-9 medium-size ripe, fresh tomatoes
     (about 2½ pounds)
 2 tablespoons minced onions
 2 tablespoons finely chopped fresh parsley
½ cup finely chopped fresh basil
 2 tablespoons butter or margarine, diced
¾ cup cubed mozzarella cheese (½-inch cubes)
¾ cup cubed Cheddar cheese (½-inch cubes)
¼ teaspoon salt
¼ teaspoon freshly ground pepper
1½ cups seasoned bread croutons

 Preheat oven to 375 degrees. Dip tomatoes in boiling water 1-2 minutes to loosen skins, peel and quarter. Put tomatoes in a saucepan and cook over medium heat 3 minutes. Remove to a greased 2-quart casserole with a slotted spoon, reserving juice for other purposes. Combine onions, parsley, basil, butter, cheeses, salt, pepper, and croutons with the tomatoes in the casserole. Bake uncovered for 20 minutes. Serve hot or at room temperature.

SERVES 4-6.

## Tomato Pudding Tallyho

15 ounces canned tomato purée
½ cup plus 1 teaspoon butter
1 teaspoon salt
1 cup light brown sugar
½ cup water
1 pound heavy textured sandwich bread,
    not too fresh

Preheat oven to 350 degrees. In a 1-quart saucepan, bring tomato purée, butter, salt, brown sugar, and water to a boil, lower heat, and simmer 10 minutes. Butter a 1½-quart casserole/server. Remove crusts from 4 slices of bread at a time, cube to 1 inch. Repeat until casserole is filled. Pour hot tomato mixture over bread cubes, stirring gently to coat each piece. Bake for 45 minutes or until a crust forms around rim. Caramelized pudding is tastiest part. Allow to cool slightly before serving in its cooking dish. May be prepared in advance and refrigerated before baking. Add 10 minutes to baking time.

SERVES 8.

**This rich treat was served as a side dish with dinner at the Tallyho Carriage House, Toledo, Ohio in the 1940s.**

## Patio Stuffed Tomatoes

6 medium tomatoes
½ pound vermicelli
¼ cup olive oil
1½ tablespoons fresh lemon juice
⅛ cup chopped chives
¼ cup mayonnaise
¼ cup sour cream
½ cup finely chopped fresh basil leaves
    salt and pepper to taste
    GARNISH:
6 whole basil leaves

Cut off tops of tomatoes, remove seeds and pulp. Drain upside down while preparing filling. Cook pasta, drain and toss with oil and lemon juice. Cool, then toss with chives, mayonnaise, sour cream, and basil. Season with salt and pepper. Spoon into tomatoes and garnish with whole basil leaves.

SERVES 6.

**A very pretty summer luncheon entrée that is especially delicious when fresh tomatoes and basil are in season.**

## Gnocchi Verdi

15  ounces frozen spinach (or 1½ pounds fresh)
1  cup ricotta cheese
2  large eggs, lightly beaten
⅔  cup freshly grated Parmesan cheese, divided
1  cup plus 3 tablespoons flour, divided
½  teaspoon salt
⅛  teaspoon pepper
⅛  teaspoon freshly grated nutmeg
3  tablespoons butter
4  cups chunky tomato sauce or tomato cream
   sauce

Cook spinach until tender. Drain well. Allow to cool. Using a wire mesh strainer, press the spinach dry with the back of a tablespoon or squeeze by hand. Chop spinach very fine and place in a medium bowl. Add ricotta cheese, eggs, one-third cup Parmesan cheese, 3 tablespoons of flour, salt, pepper, and nutmeg. Stir well. Refrigerate 30-60 minutes.

Bring a large saucepan of salted water to a boil. Spread remaining 1 cup flour in shallow baking pan. Shape a level teaspoonful of spinach-cheese mixture to form an oval. Set in baking pan of flour and roll to form a soft dough. Set aside. Continue forming oval gnocchi. Reduce water temperature to a simmer and slide gnocchi into water using a large spatula. Cook 8-12 at a time uncovered until gnocchi are slightly puffed (about 3-4 minutes) and rise to the top. Remove gnocchi with large slotted spoon, drain on a paper towel, then transfer to a buttered shallow baking dish. Continue cooking and draining gnocchi, forming a single layer in baking dish. Heat broiler. Melt butter, spoon over gnocchi. Sprinkle with remaining Parmesan cheese. Broil gnocchi 2-3 minutes until cheese topping is light brown. Serve with hot tomato sauce.

SERVES 4-6.

In a traditional Italian menu, these pasta-like dumplings would be served as a first course. Serve with beef, veal, lamb, or poultry. When entertaining, the gnocchi can be prepared a few hours in advance and then reheated.

## ROASTED TOMATOES AND ONIONS WITH SPAGHETTI

2 pounds fresh tomatoes, preferably Italian plum,
  sliced ¼ inch thick
1 large yellow onion, sliced thin
3 cloves garlic, minced
⅛ teaspoon red pepper flakes
  salt and freshly ground pepper to taste
¾ cup extra virgin olive oil
1 pound spaghetti
10 sprigs parsley, chopped

Preheat oven to 400 degrees. Arrange tomato slices in two layers in the bottom of a large shallow baking dish. Cover with sliced onions and minced garlic. Sprinkle with red pepper flakes, salt, and pepper. Pour the olive oil over all. Bake, uncovered, for about 20-25 minutes. Meanwhile, cook spaghetti al dente. Drain and place over baked sauce. Sprinkle with chopped parsley and toss well. (Variations: Add steamed, diagonally cut half-inch asparagus slices, or sautéed, sliced wild or cultivated mushrooms, or sautéed, sliced Italian sausage.)

SERVES 8.

## CREAMY PASTA LAYERS

1 pound dried pasta shells
2 pounds ground beef
2 medium onions, chopped
1 clove garlic, crushed
1 quart seasoned tomato sauce
1 pint sour cream
½ pound Provolone cheese, sliced
½ pound mozzarella cheese, sliced

Preheat oven to 350 degrees. Cook shells until barely tender; drain. In a large skillet, brown the ground beef and drain off excess fat. Add onion, garlic, and tomato sauce. Mix together and simmer for 20 minutes. Pour half of the shells in a deep casserole dish or lasagne pan and cover with half of the sauce. Spread with half of the sour cream and top with slices of Provolone cheese. Repeat the layers, ending with the mozzarella cheese on top. Cover and bake for 40-45 minutes. Remove cover and leave in oven until cheese melts and browns on top.

SERVES 8-10.

## Orecchiette Pasta with Eggplant, Zucchini, and Mushrooms

¼ cup olive oil
2 large shallots, finely minced
2 garlic cloves, finely minced
2 Japanese eggplants, sliced diagonally ¼ inch thick
2-3 small zucchini, sliced diagonally ¼ inch thick
salt
¼ pound fresh wild or cultivated mushrooms, sliced
12 fresh basil leaves
½ pound orecchiette (or other small pasta, such as shells or wheels)
olive oil to drizzle over pasta
½ pound Fontina cheese, cut in ½-inch cubes
freshly ground pepper
freshly grated Parmesan cheese

In a large skillet, heat olive oil. Sauté shallots and garlic until tender. Add eggplant and zucchini, sprinkle lightly with salt, and sauté for 2-3 minutes. Add mushrooms and basil and continue cooking for 7-9 minutes. While vegetables are sautéing, cook pasta until done. Drain well and drizzle with olive oil, tossing to coat to prevent sticking. Toss hot pasta with Fontina and sautéed vegetables; heat until cheese is hot and softened. Season to taste with salt and pepper, and sprinkle with Parmesan cheese.

SERVES 4.

The Japanese or Oriental eggplant used in this recipe is generally white and 4-5 inches long. However, the purple variety is equally good. Orecchiette or "little ears," a specialty of Apulia, Italy, is usually sold as dried pasta. It actually resembles little brimmed hats about an inch in diameter.

## Pasta alla Carbonara

1   cup thick sliced bacon, diced
¼   teaspoon minced garlic
16  ounces fresh pasta (spaghetti, fettuccine or
     linguine noodles)
3   medium sized eggs, beaten
½   cup heavy cream
½   cup grated Parmesan cheese
½   cup grated Romano cheese
     salt and freshly ground pepper to taste

 Sauté bacon and garlic over medium heat until lightly browned. Drain, cover and remove from heat. In a large pot of water, with a pinch of salt and fresh pepper added, boil the pasta until al dente. Drain thoroughly and add pasta to the bacon pan. Add eggs, cream, half the Parmesan, and half the Romano. Toss mixture until eggs turn creamy yellow. Add the remaining cheeses. Season to taste. Toss again and serve immediately.

SERVES 4.

## Pasta with Lemon Cream Sauce

1   cup heavy cream
½   cup half & half
¼   teaspoon dried hot red pepper flakes
2   tablespoons freshly grated lemon zest
14  ounces dried pasta
⅓   cup freshly grated Parmesan cheese
     salt and freshly ground pepper to taste
¼   cup fresh minced parsley

 Cook creams, red pepper, and lemon zest over low heat in a heavy saucepan for 20 minutes until mixture is reduced to about 1 cup and slightly thickened. Boil pasta according to package instructions. Drain. In a serving bowl, combine pasta, sauce, and Parmesan cheese, adding salt and pepper to taste. Sprinkle with parsley. Serve warm promptly.

SERVES 4-6.

**A delicious accompaniment to pork, veal, fish, and shrimp.**

## Vermicelli Noodle Tourte

1 tablespoon olive oil
1 pound vermicelli noodles
1 egg
¼ cup shredded Jarlsberg cheese
¼ cup shredded Cotswold or English Cheddar
   cheese
1 tablespoon smooth Dijon mustard
1 tablespoon chopped fresh thyme (or parsley)
¼ cup assorted wild mushrooms, diced and
   sautéed
   salt and pepper to taste
1 tablespoon soft butter
1 cup rich veal demi-glace (see page 101)
   combined with ¼ cup lemon juice and 1 tablespoon wild mushrooms, chopped and sautéed
18 fresh white asparagus spears, steamed
   Garnish:
   assorted wild mushrooms

 Preheat oven to 325 degrees. Fill a soup pot with water, add the oil and bring to a boil. Add the noodles and cook until al dente stage is reached. Empty into colander, run under cold water, and drain very thoroughly. Chop coarsely and transfer to a large bowl. Mix in the egg, cheeses, mustard, thyme, mushrooms, salt, and pepper. Butter 6 individual 1-cup ramekins lightly. Pack each ramekin with the noodle mixture. Place the ramekins in a baking pan, fill with 1 inch of water and cover pan with foil. Bake for 35-40 minutes or until tourtes test done when a skewer is inserted in the center. Gently heat the veal demi-glace. Unmold the individual tourtes onto the serving plates, add the white asparagus and serve with the demi-glace and the wild mushroom garnish.

Serves 6.

**Van Dyke Place Restaurant
Detroit, Michigan**

## Pecan Wild Rice Pilaf

2 cups chicken broth
½ cup wild rice, well rinsed
¾ cup water
½ cup wheat bulgar
½ cup pecan halves
½ cup dried currants
3-4 scallions, thinly sliced (white part only)
¼ cup chopped Italian parsley
¼ cup chopped fresh mint leaves
   grated zest of 1 orange
1 tablespoon orange juice
1 tablespoon olive oil
   fresh ground pepper

In a medium saucepan, bring broth to a boil. Add wild rice. Bring back to a boil, reduce heat to medium low and cook uncovered 30 minutes or until rice is tender. Do not overcook. Drain and remove to a large bowl. In another saucepan, bring water to a boil. Stir in bulgar, cover and bring back to a boil. Reduce heat to low. Simmer 15 minutes, until bulgar is tender. Remove from heat, let rest 15 minutes and then add to the wild rice. Add remaining ingredients and toss well. Serve at room temperature.

Serves 6.

**Best when made the day
before serving. Also travels
well as picnic fare.**

## RISOTTO PARMIGIANA

2   tablespoons olive oil
2   tablespoons butter
¼   cup finely chopped onion
1½  cups Arborio rice
5   cups light chicken stock, room temperature
2   tablespoons finely minced parsley (or 1 table-
     spoon dried)
6-8 tablespoons freshly grated Parmesan cheese

In a heavy 3-quart Dutch oven, heat oil and butter. Add onion and sauté until softened. Add rice and stir over medium heat for 1-2 minutes. Add about two-thirds cup of stock or enough to cover rice. Stir while cooking until all the stock is absorbed. Continue adding stock, two-thirds cup at a time, stirring and simmering (5-6 additions) until all the stock is absorbed (20-25 minutes) and the rice is tender or al dente. Add parsley. The finished dish will be creamy not runny. Stir in half the grated Parmesan cheese. Sprinkle the remainder over the top. Serve immediately. (Variation: To serve as an entrée, add one-half cup sautéed sliced mushrooms or one-half cup shredded grilled chicken or turkey.)

SERVES 4.

**The simplest of all the risottos. Authentic risotto can only be made with a short grain Arborio rice, available in Italian specialty and gourmet food shops.**

## RISOTTO WITH ASPARAGUS, TOMATO, AND SAGE

8   tablespoons unsalted butter
¼   cup minced shallots
1   clove garlic, finely minced
2   cups Arborio rice
¾   cup dry white wine
4-6 cups chicken stock, heated to a boil
1   tablespoon olive oil
1   pound small asparagus, tips only
1   cup peeled, seeded, and chopped fresh tomatoes
¾   cup grated Parmesan cheese
    GARNISH:
3-4 fresh sage leaves, chopped
     freshly ground black pepper

Melt the butter in a heavy 4-quart saucepan and sauté the shallots and garlic until tender, but not brown. Add rice and sauté until it glistens and turns opaque white (5 minutes). Add the white wine, letting it steam away as you stir. Once it has been absorbed, add one-half cup of hot stock. Cook over medium heat, stirring constantly until liquid is absorbed. Immediately add one-half cup more stock, cooking and stirring constantly. Continue adding liquid and cooking until rice is tender but still a bit firm. Keep in a warm place. Heat the olive oil in a skillet and very quickly sauté the asparagus tips (3-4 minutes). Add the tomatoes just to warm them and add to the risotto. Over low heat, stir in the cheese. If rice seems too thick, add a bit more stock. It should have a creamy consistency. Serve immediately, garnished with chopped fresh sage and black pepper.

SERVES 10-12.

Martha Stewart
Food and Entertainment Author

A birthday cake is hard to make

When you are two years old,

But I've one candle on my cake

So I'll grow strong and bold.


I'll be a baker when I'm grown

And wear a high white hat;

I'll do my baking all alone—

The dough I'll roll and pat.


I'll specialize in birthday cake—

The oven will give heat—

I'll put upon the ones I bake

Some fancy frosting sweet.


Some candles will encircle it

As many years you know

And one especially shall be lit

On which you too can grow.

# DESSERTS

## Brie and Apples in Puff Pastry

2  cups water
1  teaspoon ground cinnamon
½  teaspoon ground cloves
¾  cup sugar
2  teaspoons lemon juice
5-6  large apples
1  2-pound wheel Brie cheese
3  puff pastry sheets, 10 x 15 inches
1  egg beaten with 2 tablespoons water (egg wash)
   custard sauce (recipe follows)

Preheat oven to 375 degrees. Combine water, cinnamon, cloves, sugar, and lemon juice in a wide pot with a lid. Peel, core, and add apples; poach for 10-15 minutes. Remove apples from water. Cool and pat dry. Slice. Remove rind from Brie cheese. Slice horizontally one-eighth inch thick. Roll out puff pastry to about one-quarter inch thick. Cut 3 circles to fit a 9-inch spring-form pan. Butter bottom and sides of pan. Place first pastry circle into pan. Brush top of pastry with egg wash leaving one-eighth inch around edge unbrushed to allow pastry to rise. Arrange a single layer of poached apple slices on top of pastry to within half an inch of outside edge. Top with half of sliced Brie. Place a second pastry circle on top of apples and Brie, stretching edges of pastry to align with the first layer. Repeat egg wash, apples, and Brie. Then top with third pastry circle making certain edges are even. Pastry will be dome shaped. Brush top of pastry with egg wash, excluding edge. Decorate top with extra puff pastry cut with knife or cookie cutters. Bake for 50-55 minutes until puffed and golden brown. Serve hot or cold with custard sauce.

Custard Sauce:
3  eggs
3  tablespoons sugar
2½  cups milk
½  teaspoon vanilla extract
½  teaspoon lemon extract

In top of double boiler or in a heavy bottomed saucepan, beat eggs and sugar together lightly. Add milk. Heat and stir over a gentle heat until the sauce thickens and lightly coats the back of a spoon. Do not boil. Add extracts. Serve hot or cold.

Serves 8-10.

This impressive dessert can be produced even by a novice cook, with the help of commercially prepared puff pastry.

## Café Cream Toffee Torte

7 ounces chocolate covered toffee bars
1 quart coffee ice cream, softened
1 ounce rum or coffee-flavor liqueur
1 pound cake, cut in ½-inch slices
4 ounces bittersweet chocolate
⅓ cup toasted slivered almonds
1 quart chocolate ice cream, softened
1 ounce crème de cacao or Irish cream liqueur

In a food processor or with a rolling pin, coarsely crush toffee bars. Put half the toffee in the bottom of a 10-inch spring-form pan; set aside. Reserve other half for later use. In a large bowl, mix coffee ice cream with rum or coffee-flavor liqueur. Spoon on top of toffee layer in spring-form pan and freeze to harden. Meanwhile, prepare a layer of pound cake cut to the size of the spring-form pan; set aside. In a small pan, over hot water, melt chocolate. Stir in almonds and keep warm. Remove pan from freezer. Place pound cake over hardened ice cream and frost with chocolate almond mixture, spreading to edge of cake. Return to freezer until chocolate hardens. Meanwhile, mix chocolate ice cream and crème de cacao. Spoon on top of hardened chocolate almond layer. Sprinkle top edge with one-third of reserved crushed toffee and return to freezer. Remove from freezer 10 minutes before serving time. Run sharp knife around edges and remove sides of pan. Pat remaining crushed toffee around sides of torte.

SERVES 10-12.

## Cocoa-Mocha Layer Cake

2 cups flour
½ cup cocoa
¼ teaspoon salt
½ cup butter or margarine
1½ cups sugar
2 teaspoons baking soda
½ cup milk
1 cup boiling water
COCOA-MOCHA FROSTING:
6 tablespoons cocoa
3 cups confectioners' sugar
6 tablespoons butter, softened
1 teaspoon vanilla extract
6 tablespoons hot coffee

Preheat oven to 350 degrees. Mix together flour, cocoa, and salt; set aside. Cream butter and sugar together in large mixer bowl until lightly colored. Add baking soda to milk; add alternately with dry ingredients to creamed mixture. Add boiling water, blending well. Pour into 2 well-buttered and floured 9-inch layer pans (or 9 x 13-inch pan). Bake 30 minutes. Cool on a rack 10 minutes before removing from pans. Cool thoroughly on rack before frosting.

To prepare frosting: Blend cocoa, sugar, and butter together well. Slowly add hot coffee, stirring until a smooth, spreading consistency. Add vanilla. Fill between layers, cover top and sides of cake.

SERVES 8-10.

**Reminiscent of everyone's favorite chocolate layer cake during the 1950's.**

## "DARK VICTORY" CHOCOLATE CAKE

10 ounces butter
1 pound semi-sweet chocolate
3 tablespoons brandy
2 tablespoons flour
2 tablespoons ground nuts
1 cup sugar, divided
8 egg yolks
  pinch of salt
8 egg whites
½ cup raspberry preserves, melted and strained
  chocolate ganache (recipe follows)

Preheat oven to 400 degrees. Combine butter, chocolate, and brandy in the top of a double boiler and heat over hot (not boiling) water until chocolate is melted. Stir in flour, nuts, and one-half of the sugar. Remove from heat and cool slightly. Using an electric mixer, beat the egg yolks with salt until ribbons form. With a spatula, carefully fold in the cooled chocolate mixture. Beat the whites to soft-peak stage. Add the remaining one-half cup sugar, one tablespoon at a time and continue beating until stiff peaks form. Gently combine both mixtures with a spatula, until resulting mixture is homogeneous.

Divide batter evenly between two 9-inch buttered and floured pans. Place in the preheated oven, reduce the temperature to 350 degrees, and bake for 35 minutes. Remove from oven and cool on rack. Chill several hours. Remove from pans and glaze the tops of the cakes with the melted and strained preserves. Cover the tops with chocolate ganache. Chill to set. Remove from refrigerator and return cakes to room temperature before serving.

CHOCOLATE GANACHE:
2 tablespoons dark rum
8 ounces semi-sweet chocolate
2 tablespoons butter
1 cup heavy cream

In a double boiler over hot (not boiling) water, combine the rum, chocolate, and butter until the chocolate melts. Stir. Remove from heat and add the cream in a slow, steady stream, stirring constantly, until it is completely incorporated.

MAKES 2 CAKES, SERVES 12-16 EACH.

Elwin's Tu-Go
Royal Oak, Michigan

# "NOIR ET BLANC" POPPYSEED TORTE

**CHOCOLATE POPPYSEED LAYER:**

1   cup butter
½   cup sugar
8   egg yolks
1½  cups poppyseeds
5   ounces bittersweet chocolate, chopped and melted
7   tablespoons flour
⅔   cup ground walnuts
8   egg whites

Preheat oven to 350 degrees. Using an electric mixer, cream the butter with the sugar until light. Add the yolks, one at a time, and mix until creamy. Beat in the poppyseeds and the melted chocolate. Pour into a large bowl. Butter and flour an 8-inch spring-form pan. Mix the flour with the walnuts in a small bowl. Beat the egg whites to a soft-peak stage. Alternately fold the flour-walnut mixture and the beaten egg whites into the chocolate mixture. Pour into the spring-form pan and bake for 35-40 minutes or when done enough so that an inserted toothpick comes out clean. Cool on a rack and set aside.

**BLOND POPPYSEED LAYER:**

½   cup butter
⅔   cup sugar
1   cup poppyseeds
½   teaspoon orange zest
½   teaspoon lemon zest
2   cups flour
2   teaspoons baking powder
¼   teaspoon nutmeg
1   cup sour cream
4   egg whites

**FILLING:**

1½  cups strained apricot preserves, warm

Preheat oven to 350 degrees; butter and flour another 8-inch spring-form pan. In a mixer bowl, cream butter with the sugar until light and creamy. Beat in the poppyseeds and the zests. Sift together the flour, baking powder, and the nutmeg. Slowly mix one-third of the flour mixture into the butter mixture, and then one-third of the the sour cream into the butter mixture. Repeat process, ending with the last third of the sour cream. Transfer to a large bowl. Beat the whites to soft-peak stage and fold into the batter. Pour into the prepared pan and bake for 35-40 minutes. Cool on a rack.

To assemble torte, slice each cake in half with a serrated knife to make a total of 4 layers. Alternately stack layers on top of an 8-inch cardboard circle, spreading the top of each layer, except for the top layer, with equal amounts of the warm preserves. Press down slightly on the layers to set firmly. Coat the outside of the torte with the remaining preserves. Chill the torte in the refrigerator while preparing the ganache.

CHOCOLATE GANACHE TOPPING:
1   pound semi-sweet chocolate
2   cups heavy cream
2   tablespoons rum
    GARNISH:
6   chocolate leaves (recipe follows)
    confectioners' sugar

Melt the chocolate with the cream and rum in a double boiler on low heat. Stir to remove any lumps until a smooth consistency is achieved. Cool slightly. Remove the torte from the refrigerator, placing it on a cookie sheet. Using a ladle, pour the ganache over the torte and tilt to flow down the sides. Smooth with a spatula. Reserve any extra ganache for another use. Allow the ganache to set slightly and carefully place torte on a stand or serving plate. Place the chocolate leaves on the top in a decorative pattern and allow to completely set. Before serving, dust top with confectioners' sugar with a sifter.

CHOCOLATE LEAVES:
    medium-size leaves, such as lemon, rose, or gardenia leaves
    vegetable oil, neutral-flavored
    bittersweet or unsweetened chocolate, melted

Rub the under sides of the leaves with the oil (use a paper towel). Using a pastry brush, brush the chocolate onto the oiled surfaces and place the leaves on a sheet of waxed paper on a cookie sheet or baking pan. Place in the freezer until the chocolate is hard. Remove from the freezer and very carefully peel the real leaves away from the chocolate. Use the chocolate "leaves" to decorate the top of the torte.

SERVES 16.

Van Dyke Place
Detroit, Michigan

## TRAVERSE CITY CHERRY BERRY PIE

## CHOCOLATE DERBY PIE

2  unbaked 9-inch pie crusts
10  ounces frozen raspberries, thawed
3  tablespoons cornstarch
½  teaspoon salt
¾  cup sugar
2  cups pitted fresh red tart cherries
½  teaspoon ground cinnamon
1  quart vanilla or cinnamon ice cream

¼  cup flour
1  cup sugar
2  large eggs, slightly beaten
½  cup butter or margarine, melted and cooled
1  cup chopped pecans
6  ounces semi-sweet chocolate chips
1  teaspoon vanilla
1  (9-inch) unbaked pie crust
GARNISH:
1  cup whipped cream
½  cup chocolate shavings

Preheat oven to 425 degrees. Line a pie plate with one of the pie crusts. Drain raspberries, reserving syrup. Add water to syrup to make 1 cup. In a saucepan, combine the cup of liquid with the cornstarch, salt, and sugar. When cornstarch is dissolved, add the cherries. Cook over low heat, stirring, until mixture is thick and clear. Stir in raspberries and cinnamon. Pour filling into pastry shell. Top with second crust, crimping the edge and venting the top. Bake for 30 minutes or until the filling is hot and the crust is golden. Cool and serve with a scoop of ice cream.

SERVES 6-8.

Preheat oven to 350 degrees. In medium-size bowl, mix flour and sugar. Add eggs, melted butter, pecans, chocolate, and vanilla. Mix with wire whisk. Pour into unbaked pie shell. Bake 45 minutes. Garnish each slice with a dollop of whipped cream and chocolate shavings.

SERVES 8.

**Traverse City is the capital of Michigan's fabulous cherry-producing region.**

## Pumpkin Custard Cream Pie

¾ cup milk
2 cups pumpkin
1½ cups brown sugar
⅛ teaspoon salt
¾ teaspoon ginger
¾ teaspoon cinnamon
⅓ teaspoon nutmeg
5 egg yolks
½ ounce (2 tablespoons) unflavored gelatin
⅓ cup cold water
5 egg whites
1½ cups heavy cream
⅓ cup sugar
1 baked 10-inch baked pie shell

Garnish:
caramelized almonds (recipe follows)
¼-½ cup butterscotch sauce
whipped cream

Before serving, sprinkle each piece with caramelized almonds, drizzle with butterscotch sauce, and top with whipped cream

Heat milk, pumpkin, brown sugar, salt, and spices. Beat egg yolks slightly and add hot mixture to yolks. Mix well and cook in double boiler until thick, stirring constantly. Soften gelatin in cold water and add to hot custard. Stir until dissolved. Cool until custard begins to thicken. Beat egg whites until stiff, but not dry. Fold in custard. Cool a little while, but not until set. Whip cream. Fold the sugar into whipped cream, then fold cream into pumpkin mixture. Chill until very thick and pour into baked pie shell. Chill 2 hours.

Caramelized Almonds:
½ cup sugar
1 cup slivered blanched almonds

Stir sugar and almonds constantly in heavy skillet until caramel color. Spread on cookie sheet. Break apart when crisp. These keep indefinitely in an air-tight container. (Can be used on ice cream, etc.)

Serves 8.

## BAVARIAN APPLE CHEESECAKE

CRUST:
½  cup butter
⅓  cup sugar
¼  teaspoon vanilla
¼  teaspoon grated nutmeg
1  cup flour

Cream butter and sugar together in electric mixer bowl. Add vanilla, beat well. Stir nutmeg into flour, gradually add to creamed mixture beating just until blended. Gather dough and pat into the bottom and sides of a 9 x 1½-inch spring-form pan. Set aside.

FILLING:
8  ounces cream cheese, room temperature
¼  cup sugar
1  egg, room temperature
½  teaspoon vanilla

In mixer bowl, beat together cream cheese, sugar, egg, and vanilla until smooth. Set aside.

TOPPING:
4  apples, peeled, cored, thinly sliced (4 cups)
½  cup sugar
1  tablespoon grated orange zest
1  teaspoon ground cinnamon
¼  cup sliced almonds

Preheat oven to 450 degrees. Toss together apple slices, sugar, orange zest, and cinnamon. Pour filling into prepared crust. Arrange apple slices over the filling in an overlapping circular pattern. Sprinkle almonds over the top. Bake for 10 minutes then reduce heat to 400 degrees and bake an additional 25 minutes. Allow to cool in pan before slicing.

SERVES 8.

The perfect combination—apples, cream cheese, and almonds.

## DOUBLE CHOCOLATE-WALNUT BROWNIES

1 cup butter or margarine
4 ounces unsweetened chocolate
2 cups sugar
3 eggs (or 5 egg whites), room temperature
1 teaspoon vanilla extract
1 cup flour
1½ cups chopped English or black walnuts
6 ounces semi-sweet chocolate pieces

Preheat oven to 350 degrees. Melt butter and chocolate in top of a double boiler over simmering water. Remove from heat and pour into a medium mixing bowl. Stir to blend. Using a wooden spoon, beat in sugar gradually until combined. Add eggs, one at a time, beating after each addition. Stir in vanilla. Using a rubber spatula or wooden spoon, fold in flour until thoroughly combined. Stir in 1 cup walnuts. Spread into a greased 13 x 9 x 2-inch pan. Combine remaining one-half cup walnuts and chocolate pieces, sprinkle over top of batter. Bake for 35 minutes. Remove and cool in pan before cutting into squares.

MAKES 2-3 DOZEN.

**The best of the best!**

## FRESH APPLE NUT CAKE

2⅓ cups flour
2 cups sugar
2 teaspoons baking soda
¾ teaspoon salt
1 teaspoon cinnamon
¼ teaspoon ground ginger
¼ teaspoon ground cloves
4 cups shredded or finely chopped apples
½ cup margarine or butter, room temperature
½ cup chopped walnuts or pecans
2 large eggs, lightly beaten
1 teaspoon vanilla
confectioners' sugar

Preheat oven to 350 degrees. In a large mixer bowl, blend flour, sugar, baking soda, salt, cinnamon, ginger, and cloves. Add the shredded apples, margarine or butter, nuts, eggs, and vanilla to the dry ingredients. Mix at medium speed until thoroughly blended. Batter will be stiff. Pour into a greased and floured 9 x 13 x 2-inch pan. Bake 40-45 minutes, or until a toothpick inserted comes out clean. Cool completely on a rack. Dust lightly with powdered sugar. To serve, cut into 3-inch squares.

SERVES 12.

This simple, old-fashioned cake can become a festive dessert when accompanied by ice cream topped with praline or caramel sauce.

## PECAN DIAMONDS

5 tablespoons unsalted butter
1½ tablespoons vegetable shortening
4½ tablespoons sugar
1 egg
½ teaspoon vanilla
1½ cups flour
    pinch of baking powder
    pinch of salt
    FILLING:
1 cup unsalted butter
½ cup honey
1¼ cups brown sugar
¼ cup granulated sugar
4 cups pecans, chopped
¼ cup heavy cream

Preheat oven to 350 degrees. In mixer bowl, cream butter, shortening, and sugar; add egg and vanilla until blended. Combine flour, baking powder, and salt and add gradually. Wrap dough and set aside for 30 minutes. Grease a 9 x 13 x 2-inch pan. Roll or pat dough and fit to cover bottom and sides of pan. Bake for 3 minutes. To prepare filling, combine butter, honey, and sugars in saucepan. Bring to a boil and cook for 3 minutes or until slightly thickened. Remove and cool. Fold in pecans and cream. Pour into the prebaked shell. Bake at 350 degrees for 30 minutes. Remove and set to cool. Cut into diamonds.

MAKES 3 DOZEN.

## PATINA DI NATALE

3 cups flour
2 teaspoons baking powder
    pinch of salt
1 cup butter, diced
½ cup chopped pine nuts
1 cup plus 2 tablespoons sugar
2 eggs
    grated zest of 1 lemon
1 egg yolk mixed with ½ tablespoon water for glaze

Preheat oven to 425 degrees. Sift together, flour, baking powder, and salt in large bowl. Add butter to flour mixture, break with fork until texture resembles coarse meal. Add pine nuts. In separate bowl, beat sugar and eggs together. Add lemon zest. Mix dry ingredients with egg-sugar mixture until dough is firm. Knead 1-2 minutes. Divide dough into quarters and wrap in plastic wrap. Chill 1 hour. Roll out one piece at a time, cut into desired shape with cookie cutters. Arrange on ungreased baking sheet. Brush glaze on each cookie with pastry brush. Bake for 10 minutes until lightly golden. Remove to cooling rack.

MAKES 3 DOZEN.

**A traditional Italian butter cookie flavored with lemon and pine nuts.**

## Oatmeal Chunkies

1 cup butter or margarine, softened
1 cup brown sugar
1 cup white sugar
2 eggs
1 teaspoon vanilla
½ teaspoon lemon extract
1½ cups flour
1 teaspoon salt
1 teaspoon baking soda
3 cups quick-cooking oats
½ cup chopped walnuts or pecans
½ cup coconut

Cream butter or margarine together with brown and white sugar. In a separate bowl, beat eggs thoroughly, and blend into creamed mixture. Add vanilla and lemon extracts, mixing well. Combine flour, salt, and baking soda and stir into batter. Add oats, nuts, and coconut. Batter will be stiff. Divide equally and roll into 4 logs approximately 9 inches long. Wrap and refrigerate 1 hour. Preheat oven to 350 degrees. Cut chilled logs into one-half-inch slices. Place on greased cookie sheet. Bake for 10-12 minutes until lightly browned. Allow to cool on cookie sheet 2-3 minutes before removing.

MAKES 6 DOZEN.

**A milk-and-cookies favorite.**

## Raspberry Triangles

¾ cup butter
1 cup sugar
1 egg
1 teaspoon vanilla
¼ teaspoon salt
2 cups flour
1 cup grated coconut
½ cup chopped walnuts
1 cup raspberry jam

Preheat oven to 350 degrees. In a mixer bowl, cream butter and sugar together until light. Add egg, vanilla, salt and blend. Fold in flour, coconut, and walnuts. Press three-quarters of the batter into a greased 13 x 9 x 2-inch pan. Spread jam over dough evenly. Top with remaining dough, arranging pieces in a pattern so the jam shows. Bake for 30 minutes. Remove and cool completely before cutting into triangles.

MAKES 2 DOZEN.

## BERRIES AND RUSSIAN CREAM

½ cup water
¼ ounce (1 tablespoon) unflavored gelatin
½ cup sugar
1 cup light cream
1 cup sour cream
½ teaspoon vanilla
TOPPING:
2 cups sliced strawberries, or whole raspberries or blueberries
1 tablespoon sugar
1 tablespoon Grand Marnier liqueur

Pour one-half cup water in a small bowl and sprinkle with gelatin. Stir to blend. Set the bowl in a pan of boiling water and dissolve gelatin. Mix together sugar and heavy cream in a small saucepan. Heat until sugar is dissolved. Stir in gelatin and allow mixture to cool to room temperature. Add sour cream and vanilla. Beat until smooth. Pour into 8 individual dishes or tall stem glasses and refrigerate for 2 hours. Mix together berries, sugar, and liqueur. Refrigerate. At serving, ladle berry topping over each portion.

SERVES 8.

**A rich but refreshing way to feature fresh berries when they are in season.**

## CHOCO-MINT MOUSSECUPS

3 egg whites
15 square soda crackers, crushed
1 cup chopped pecans
1 cup sugar
2 teaspoons vanilla, divided
1½ cups butter, softened
3 cups confectioners' sugar
6 ounces semi-sweet chocolate, melted and cooled
6 eggs
1½ teaspoons peppermint extract
GARNISH:
1 pint whipped cream
24 maraschino or candied stemmed cherries
24 mint leaves

Preheat oven to 325 degrees. Beat egg whites until stiff. Fold in crackers, pecans, sugar, and 1 teaspoon vanilla until blended. Spoon 1 tablespoon of mixture into 24 foil cupcake liners. Bake for 20 minutes. Remove and set aside. Using electric mixer, beat butter until light and fluffy, adding confectioners' sugar gradually. Beat for 5 minutes. Pour in melted chocolate and continue to beat an additional 3 minutes. Add eggs, one at a time, beating well after each addition. Add remaining teaspoon vanilla and peppermint extract. Beat additional 5 minutes. Fill each cup to the top with chocolate mixture. Freeze until ready to serve. At serving time, garnish each cup with whipped cream, a maraschino stemmed cherry, and small mint leaf. Refrigerate 15-30 minutes before serving to soften.

SERVES 24.

**With these in the freezer you're prepared for even unexpected guests.**

## Black Beast Dessert

8   ounces unsweetened chocolate
4   ounces semi-sweet chocolate
1⅓  cups sugar
½   cup water
1   cup unsalted butter, room temperature
5   eggs, room temperature

Chocolate Ganache:
1   cup heavy cream
10  ounces semi-sweet or bittersweet chocolate
    pieces
2   tablespoons Grand Marnier liqueur or brandy
Garnish:
1½  pints fresh berries

 Preheat oven to 350 degrees. Grease well an 8 or 9-inch cake pan and line the bottom with greased parchment paper. In a food processor, chop chocolate into small pieces using a number of short pulses (following machine instructions). Bring sugar and water to a boil in saucepan, remove. Carefully pour into processor with chocolate and process until blended. Add butter, and process again until blended. Add eggs to mixture, one at a time, with the machine running. Pour mixture into cake pan and set in a pan large enough to hold the cake pan. Add boiling water to reach halfway up cake pan. Bake for 30 minutes. Remove cake pan from water bath and cool on a rack. Unmold, only when completely cooled, by inverting onto a serving plate covered with wax paper strips. Refrigerate cake.

In a saucepan, bring heavy cream to a boil, add chocolate pieces, and whisk over medium heat until smooth. Add liqueur. Allow to cool to room temperature. Pour one-half of ganache over cake, allowing it to run over the sides of cake. Refrigerate 10 minutes until ganache begins to set. Repeat process with remaining ganache. Decorative swirls can be made with a cake knife or spatula. Remove protective wax paper strips. Refrigerate. Allow cake to stand at room temperature 30 minutes before serving. Arrange whole berries around edge of cake and garnish each slice with the extras.

Serves 24.

The ultimate dessert for chocolate lovers! Although this recipe uses a food processor, the chocolate can easily be chopped with a chef's knife, and the batter blended with an electric mixer.

## Chocolate Pâté

2   *large eggs*
8   *ounces sweet cooking chocolate*
⅓   *cup butter*
1   *tablespoon instant coffee*
2   *tablespoons dark rum*
1   *teaspoon vanilla*
1½   *cups finely ground walnuts*
2   *cups heavy cream*
   *raspberry sauce (recipe follows)*

RASPBERRY SAUCE:
10   *ounces fresh or frozen raspberries*
2   *tablespoons crème de cassis liqueur or kirsch brandy*
   *sugar to taste*

 Line the entire surface of an 8 x 4 x 2-inch loaf pan with plastic wrap with ends extending over edges of pan. In a small bowl, beat eggs until yolks and whites are blended. In a double boiler over hot water, melt chocolate and butter, stirring often. Stir in instant coffee and rum, and continue stirring until coffee is dissolved. Add eggs and stir constantly until slightly thickened. Remove from heat, stir in vanilla and walnuts. Turn into large bowl and cool to room temperature. Whip cream until stiff, fold into chocolate mixture. Turn into prepared pan. Chill for 6-8 hours or overnight.

Purée berries in a blender or food processor. Sieve fruit through a strainer. Add liqueur and sugar to taste, if needed. To serve, lift loaf from pan and slice thin. Spoon raspberry sauce in bottom of individual dessert plates, top with a slice of pâté. Pâté may also be spread on thin ginger crackers or lemon wafers.

SERVES 16.

**Just a little goes a long way!**

## COMPANY'S COMING FRUIT FLAN

6   ounces vanilla wafers (processed into fine
    crumbs)
4   ounces ground pecans
¾   cup melted butter or margarine
2   large eggs, beaten
½   cup sugar
1   tablespoon vanilla
8   ounces cream cheese
½   cup sour cream
2   kiwi, peeled, sliced thin
2   peaches, peeled, sliced thin
1   pint fresh strawberries, hulled and sliced
4   ounces apple jelly

Preheat oven to 375 degrees. In a 9-inch spring-form, flan, or pie pan, mix together wafer crumbs and ground nuts. Stir in melted butter and shape or mold crumb mixture to line the pan evenly. Set aside. In a mixer bowl, beat eggs until well blended. With the machine running, slowly add sugar, vanilla, and cream cheese. Beat well for 2 minutes. Add sour cream and continue to beat. When well blended, pour filling into prepared crust and bake for 35 minutes. Remove when filling is solid and lightly golden, and when a knife blade inserted comes out clean. Cool completely on a rack. Refrigerate or freeze until day of serving. (To freeze, wrap well and keep no longer than 2-3 weeks.) At least two hours before serving, remove flan from freezer or refrigerator. Arrange the fruit slices overlapping each other in rows. Melt apple jelly and brush on fruit, allowing excess to fill cracks, covering entire surface. Refrigerate until glaze is set.

SERVES 6-8.

## FROZEN MOCHA MOUSSE

½   cup sugar
5   egg yolks
3   tablespoons coffee flavored liqueur
2   tablespoons lukewarm espresso or French
    roasted black coffee
2   cups heavy cream
    GARNISH:
3   ounces chocolate shavings or chocolate curls

In the top of a double boiler over simmering water, beat together egg yolks and sugar, using a wire whisk or hand mixer, until mixture is thick and flows slowly from the beaters. Add liqueur and coffee and whisk or beat again until thickened. Remove pan from heat and continue beating until mixture has cooled. In a separate bowl beat cream until it mounds in soft peaks. Fold whipped cream into egg mixture with a rubber spatula. Spoon into individual 4-ounce soufflé dishes. Garnish with chocolate shavings. Freeze for 4 hours before serving. Serve frozen.

SERVES 6.

A simple, rich, and elegant dessert.

Snow comes and goes,

And then it snows

Again.

Gay flowers will come

And bees all hum,

But when?

# Breakfast
# &
# Brunch

## APPLE-BERRY SMOOTHIE

1   *banana, peeled, cut in chunks*
1   *medium apple, cored and diced*
6-7   *strawberries, washed, hulled*
1   *cup kefir, raspberry or strawberry flavored*
2   *cups fresh apple cider*

Put fruit in a blender. Purée for 60 seconds or until smooth. Add kefir and cider. Purée for 30 seconds. Serve immediately.

SERVES 4-6.

**One of the main ingredients in this healthy breakfast drink is kefir, a cultured milk similar to yogurt, available in health food stores.**

## APPLE TEA PUNCH

8   *cups orange pekoe or English breakfast tea*
1   *cup apple juice*
½   *cup orange juice*
1   *(3-inch) cinnamon stick, crushed*
1   *(3-inch) strip fresh orange peel*
2   *whole star anise*
    GARNISH:
2-3   *sprigs of fresh mint*

Cool freshly steeped tea to room temperature. Add apple juice, orange juice, cinnamon, orange peel, and anise. Refrigerate 3-4 hours. Remove spices. Serve with ice and garnish with mint sprigs. In winter, heat tea, juices, and spices together in a saucepan until punch just begins to simmer. Remove from heat and serve immediately. Remove spices before serving.

SERVES 12.

**An all-season punch recipe which is equally pleasing whether served hot or cold.**

## "No Nothing" Waffles

3   *eggs whites, room temperature*
1   *cup flour*
1   *cup skim milk*
3   *tablespoons corn oil*

Beat egg whites until stiff. Mix flour, milk, and oil. Fold egg whites into batter. If nonstick waffle iron is not used, brush surface with corn oil. Preheat waffle iron, then add batter and bake until golden. Serve with a sugar-free fruit syrup.

SERVES 2.

These waffles have no cholesterol, no salt, and no sugar—nothing but good taste.

## Farmers Cheese Pancakes

½   *cup flour*
⅛   *teaspoon salt*
½   *teaspoon baking powder*
2   *tablespoons sugar*
1   *heaping tablespoon bran or wheat germ*
8   *ounces farmers cheese or cottage cheese*
2   *eggs*
¼   *cup milk*
    *grated zest of 2 oranges or lemons*
    *margarine or oil for cooking pancakes*

In a medium mixing bowl, blend together flour, salt, baking powder, sugar, and bran or wheat germ. Add cheese, eggs, and milk. Stir, then allow to set while grating the oranges or lemons. Add zest and mix. Consistency should be thick. If too thin, add another tablespoon of bran. Heat 2 tablespoons margarine or oil in a large frying pan. Ladle batter in 3-inch circles. Cook until browned on one side. Turn over and finish other side.

SERVES 2.

This hearty breakfast dish can be enjoyed any time of the day. Serve with lingon-berry or raspberry jam.

## CHEESY POPOVER RING

1   cup water
½   cup butter or margarine
1   teaspoon salt
⅛   teaspoon pepper
1   cup flour
4   eggs
1   cup shredded sharp Cheddar cheese

 Preheat oven to 425 degrees. Mix together water, butter, salt, and pepper in a saucepan and bring to a boil. Add flour all at once, beating well. Remove from heat, add eggs one at a time, mixing well after each addition. Remove 2 tablespoons cheese and set aside. Stir remaining cheese into flour mixture. Drop dough by rounded tablespoonfuls onto a greased baking sheet to form an 8-inch ring. Sprinkle reserved cheese on top. Bake for 45 minutes or until golden brown. Serve hot.

SERVES 4-6.

## THE BEST BUTTERMILK PANCAKES

2   cups flour
½   teaspoon salt
1   teaspoon baking soda
1   tablespoon sugar
2   eggs
2   cups buttermilk
⅛   cup butter or margarine, melted

 In a large mixing bowl, sift together flour, salt, baking soda, and sugar. Beat the eggs until light. Add the buttermilk and melted butter. Combine the sifted flour mixture with the egg mixture just until blended. Do not overmix. Cook by dropping large spoonfuls on hot buttered griddle over medium heat. Turn pancakes once, after edges are lightly browned and pancake surface forms tiny air holes.

SERVES 3-4.

## SMOKED SALMON AND WILD MUSHROOM
## CHEESECAKE

  1    *cup chopped leeks*
  8    *tablespoons butter, divided*
 ¼    *cup sliced fresh wild mushrooms*
       *(shiitake, chanterelle, trumpet)*
       *(or substitute button if not available)*
1¼  *pounds cream cheese*
  4    *egg yolks*
  1    *tablespoon cornstarch*
 ⅓    *cup heavy cream*
 ¼    *pound smoked salmon*
 ½    *cup grated Swiss-type cheese*
 ¼    *cup chopped, toasted walnuts*
 ¼    *cup crushed wheat crackers*
 ¼    *cup fresh grated Romano cheese*
       GARNISH:
       *sliced tomatoes*
       *slightly whipped cream*

Preheat oven to 300 degrees. In skillet, sauté the leeks in 3 tablespoons of the butter until tender. Increase the heat to medium-high and add the mushrooms. When mushrooms are cooked, remove the mixture to a plate using a slotted spoon. Cool to room temperature. In a food processor or electric mixer, blend the cream cheese, egg yolks, corn starch, and heavy cream until smooth. Cut the smoked salmon into julienne strips. Combine it with the grated Swiss cheese, leek-mushroom mixture, and cream cheese mixture. Melt the rest of the butter. In a small bowl, combine the nuts, cracker crumbs, and Romano cheese. Add the melted butter and mix. Press into the bottom and one-quarter inch up the sides of a 9 or 10-inch spring-form pan. Carefully pour the filling into the prepared pan. Tap the pan gently on the counter to remove any air bubbles. Place the pan into a large roasting pan and fill with hot water to reach half way up the sides of the larger pan. Place in the oven for 1½ hours. Turn off the heat and leave the cake in the oven for an additional hour.

Remove the cake pan from the water. Let it come to room temperature. Chill overnight. The next day, unmold the cake (place it in a shallow pan of hot water to loosen it from the pan). Slice the cake while it is still cold. Serve the slices at room temperature, garnished with sliced tomatoes and slightly whipped cream, if desired.

MAKES 12-16 APPETIZER SERVINGS.

**Elwin's Tu-Go**
**Royal Oak, Michigan**

## Herb Omelet Torte

20-24 ounces frozen puff pastry
(defrosted 15 minutes)
FILLING:
1 tablespoon olive oil
1 tablespoon butter
1 garlic clove, minced
1 pound spinach leaves, rinsed, stems removed,
and dried
½ teaspoon freshly grated nutmeg
salt and pepper to taste
12 ounces Swiss cheese, shredded
½ pound cooked ham, turkey, or chicken, thinly
sliced
2 red peppers, cut into strips, sautéed
(or 4 ounces pimentos, drained)
12 black olives, pitted and sliced
1 egg, beaten

Lightly butter an 8 or 9-inch spring-form pan. Roll out puff pastry one-quarter inch thick. Line bottom and sides of pan with the pastry. Seal pastry seams by moistening with a few dabs of water and pressing together. Reserve enough dough to cut a large circle to cover top and to decorate. Refrigerate pan and pastry circle for top.

To prepare omelet filling: Heat olive oil and butter in a large skillet. Add garlic and spinach, sauté together until wilted. Continue heating until water is evaporated. Season with nutmeg, salt, and pepper. Remove to a plate and refrigerate.

OMELET:
6 eggs
1 ½ tablespoons chopped chives or green onion
2 tablespoons chopped parsley
1 tablespoon snipped dill weed
1 tablespoon chopped tarragon
salt and pepper to taste
2 tablespoons butter

Beat together the eggs, herbs, salt, and pepper. Heat 1 tablespoon butter in an 8 or 10-inch skillet over medium heat. Pour one-half of the egg mixture into skillet. Be sure to loosen edges while omelet is cooking. When set, remove omelet to a platter. Cook a second omelet with remaining butter and egg mixture.

To assemble torte: Preheat oven to 350 degrees. Remove spring-form pan from refrigerator. Layer in pan 1 omelet, one-half of the cooked spinach, one-half of the shredded cheese, and one-half of the meat. Add all the red pepper and olives. Repeat layering in reverse order using remaining ingredients. Cover omelet with reserved pastry circle and seal to side pastry by pinching dough together with fingers. With the tip of a paring knife, evenly mark 8 slits in the pastry top. Brush with beaten egg. Set pan on a cookie sheet. Bake 50-60 minutes. Cool slightly before removing from pan and slicing. Serve hot or at room temperature.

SERVES 8.

## ZUCCHINI SAUSAGE PIE

4 tablespoons butter, divided
2 tablespoons chopped onion
2 cups shredded zucchini
½ pound sweet Italian sausage, cut in chunks
1 baked 9-inch pastry shell
1 cup shredded Swiss cheese
4 eggs
½ cup heavy cream
¼ cup grated Parmesan cheese
¼ teaspoon salt
¼ teaspoon ground white pepper
¼ teaspoon ground nutmeg

Preheat oven to 450 degrees. In a skillet, heat 2 tablespoons butter and sauté onion, remove from pan when lightly golden. Add more butter and sauté zucchini for 5 minutes. Remove zucchini and drain. Cook sausage in remaining butter. Remove and drain on towelling, then crumble. Spread zucchini and onion on bottom of pastry shell. Sprinkle with sausage pieces, then Swiss cheese. Beat eggs lightly. Add cream, Parmesan cheese, salt, and pepper. Pour into pastry shell and sprinkle with nutmeg. Bake for 15 minutes, reduce temperature to 350 degrees and bake 10 minutes or until center is firm. Let stand for 10 minutes before serving.

SERVES 6.

## CHICKEN AND ASPARAGUS QUICHE

1 unbaked 8 or 9-inch pie shell
¾ cup finely diced cooked chicken
¼ cup finely diced ham
2 cups cut cooked asparagus, ½-inch pieces
1 cup shredded Swiss cheese
3 eggs
milk or light cream
pinch of nutmeg
pinch of pepper
GARNISH:
6 whole cooked asparagus spears

Preheat oven to 425 degrees. Into unbaked pie shell, place chicken, ham, asparagus, and Swiss cheese. Break 3 eggs into a large measuring cup, add enough milk or cream to make 1¼ cups. Add pinch each of nutmeg and pepper. Beat well with fork. Pour over mixture in pie shell. Decorate with cooked asparagus spears. Bake for 15 minutes. Reduce heat to 300 degrees and bake 30-40 minutes, or until cold knife inserted into center comes out clean.

SERVES 6-8.

There is nothing finer than the very first spring crop of Michigan asparagus.

## Spanakopita (Spinach Pie)

¼  cup olive oil
½  cup finely chopped onion
¼  cup finely chopped scallions
 2  pounds spinach leaves, washed, trimmed
¼  cup finely cut fresh dill weed (or 2 tablespoons
    dried)
¼  cup chopped parsley
    freshly ground pepper and nutmeg to taste
¾  pound feta cheese, crumbled
¾  pound dry cottage or farmers cheese, crumbled
 5  eggs, lightly beaten
10  sheets frozen filo dough, thawed
½  cup melted butter for brushing dough

Heat oil in skillet, sauté onion and scallions until soft. Stir in the spinach, cover tightly for 5 minutes. Drain spinach and chop. Add the dill, parsley, pepper, and nutmeg. In a mixing bowl, blend cheeses and eggs. Add the spinach mixture. Preheat oven to 350 degrees. Butter a 9 x 13-inch baking dish. Set a dampened cloth or towel on counter top. Unfold dough. Brush 4 sheets of filo with melted butter. Fit each inside baking pan, covering corners and sides. Fill with spinach mixture. Spread evenly. Cover with remaining filo sheets brushed with melted butter, one at a time, tucking in corners. Brush top sheet with butter and bake 40-50 minutes until center is hot and top is golden brown.

Serves 8-10.

## Night Before Brunch Bake

3  cups ham, sausage, or Canadian bacon, cooked
   and cubed
3  cups French bread, cubed
3  cups shredded sharp Cheddar cheese
3  tablespoons flour
5  tablespoons melted butter or margarine
¼  teaspoon dry mustard
   dash of Tabasco sauce or cayenne pepper
5  eggs
2  cups milk

In a large mixing bowl, combine meat, bread, and cheese. In a separate bowl, mix together flour, melted butter, and seasonings. Stir into meat mixture. Mix well. In a small bowl, slightly beat eggs and stir in milk. Pour over meat mixture. Mix until blended. Pour into a 13 x 9-inch baking dish. Cover and refrigerate overnight. Bake uncovered at 350 degrees for 55-60 minutes. If not prepared in advance and refrigerated, reduce baking time 10 minutes.

Serves 6-8.

This traditional favorite can be reduced in cholesterol by using commercial egg substitute, low-fat cheese, and margarine.

## BAKED HAM LOAF WITH MUSTARD SAUCE

1½   pounds ground ham
1½   pounds fresh ground pork
1½   cups dried seasoned bread crumbs
½   cup chopped onion
2   eggs, beaten
½   cup milk
    MUSTARD SAUCE:
1   egg, beaten
⅓   cup sugar
¼   cup dry mustard
½   cup vinegar
    salt (optional)
¾   cup mayonnaise

Preheat oven to 350 degrees. In a large bowl, mix together ground ham, ground pork, bread crumbs, onion, eggs, and milk. Turn mixture into a large 10 x 5-inch loaf pan or 2 smaller 7 x 3½-inch pans. Bake for 1-1½ hours depending upon pan size.

While ham loaf is baking, prepare mustard sauce. Using a double boiler, mix egg, sugar, mustard, vinegar, and a pinch of salt over hot or simmering water. Stir until mixture slightly thickens. Remove from heat and allow to cool 1 hour. Add mayonnaise and blend until smooth. When ham loaf is cooked, cool slightly before slicing. Arrange on a serving plate and pour mustard sauce over the top.

SERVES 6.

## PHYLLO ARTICHOKE PIE

1   cup shredded Gruyère cheese
½   cup shredded Swiss cheese
1   pound low-fat ricotta cheese
3   eggs, beaten
½   cup light sour cream
24   ounces marinated artichoke hearts, drained, quartered
½   cup diced red pepper
3   tablespoons fresh basil leaves
½   cup sliced green onions
    salt and freshly ground pepper to taste
10-12   sheets phyllo dough
½   pound melted butter
½   cup grated Parmesan cheese mixed with 1 teaspoon paprika and 3 tablespoons bread crumbs

Preheat oven to 400 degrees. Mix Gruyère, Swiss, and ricotta cheeses. Add beaten eggs and sour cream. Add artichoke hearts, red pepper, basil, green onions, salt, and pepper. Butter bottom and sides of 9 x 13-inch baking dish. Brush 4 sheets of phyllo with melted butter. Sprinkle each sheet with Parmesan bread crumb mixture. Place individually in baking dish so that sheets extend over sides of dish. Pour in filling. Spread evenly. Brush remaining sheets with butter, sprinkle with Parmesan bread crumbs, and fold in half. Lay on top of mixture, fold extended ends over folded sheets. Brush top with butter. Bring ingredients to room temperature. Bake for 25-30 minutes. May be frozen.

SERVES 8-10.

## RATATOUILLE PIE

CRUST:

3  cups flour
½  teaspoon salt
1  cup corn oil margarine, diced
1  egg yolk, lightly beaten
¼-½  cup water

FILLING:

2  large onions, sliced
3-4  tablespoons olive oil
3  green peppers, sliced
1  medium eggplant, unpeeled, cubed 1 inch
1  medium zucchini, cubed 1 inch
3  large cloves garlic, finely minced
4  large tomatoes, peeled, seeded, and cubed
1  teaspoon dried basil
   (or 1 tablespoon chopped fresh)
   salt and pepper to taste
½  cup chopped fresh parsley
½  cup shredded mozzarella cheese
1  cup grated Parmesan cheese

In a bowl, mix together flour and salt. Add margarine, breaking up cubes with a fork until texture resembles small pebbles. Stir in yolk. Add one-quarter cup water, stirring dough until it gathers. Add more water if needed. Divide dough into 2 parts, wrap and refrigerate 2-3 hours or overnight. On a lightly floured surface, roll dough one-quarter inch thick and fit into two 8 or 9-inch pie pans, reserving the extra for lattice top. Refrigerate while preparing the filling.

In a large skillet, sauté onions in olive oil until soft. Add peppers. When they begin to soften, add eggplant, zucchini, and garlic. Cook uncovered over medium heat about 15 minutes. Add tomatoes and basil and continue cooking 5-10 minutes. Season with salt and pepper. Add parsley. Remove from heat and cool to lukewarm. Preheat oven to 400 degrees. Add mozzarella cheese to vegetable mixture. Spoon into pie shells and cover each with grated Parmesan. Top with pastry lattice, sealing strips with egg white. Bake 40-45 minutes.

To freeze unbaked pie, wrap in heavy duty foil or freezer paper. Bake frozen at 400 degrees for 45-50 minutes.

MAKES 2 PIES, 6-8 SERVINGS EACH.

This double recipe allows you to freeze one pie unbaked for a second impressive meal later.

## Blossom Fruit Cup

1   whole pineapple, peeled, cored
4   seedless oranges, peeled, cut in segments
½   cup dried cranberries or dried cherries
¼-½ cup Grand Marnier liqueur
1   star fruit

 Slice fresh pineapple, then cut into chunks. Remove all pith from orange segments. In a mixing bowl, toss pineapple chunks, orange segments, and dried cranberries, adding Grand Marnier to taste. At serving time, peel the star fruit, slice, and arrange on the fruit salad. Serve chilled.

Serves 6.

## Citrus Butter

1   whole tangerine
1   whole lime
1½  cups sugar
2   cups (1 pound) unsalted butter, room
    temperature

 Quarter the fruit, remove seeds, and purée in a food processor or blender. Add sugar and softened butter, blend well. Remove and store in tightly covered butter crocks or ceramic bowls. Keep refrigerated up to 2 weeks or freeze.

Makes about 3 cups.

**The refreshing, mild fruit flavor is delicious on warm toast or croissants.**

# Pommes Charlotte

6-7 slices homemade-style white bread, crusts
  trimmed
3 large cooking apples, peeled, cored, thinly
  sliced
1 tablespoon butter
2 tablespoons brown sugar
½ teaspoon cinnamon
¼ teaspoon ground allspice
  extra cinnamon for sprinkling
¾ cup melted, unsalted butter

TOPPING:
1 tablespoon brown sugar
¼ teaspoon cinnamon
⅛ teaspoon ground allspice
⅛ teaspoon ground cloves

 Preheat oven to 350 degrees. Cut two of the bread slices into circles to fit the top and bottom of a number 14 charlotte mold (available in gourmet shops). Cut remaining bread into fingers 1½ x 3 inches. Sauté apple slices in 1 tablespoon butter until tender and lightly golden. Mix brown sugar, cinnamon, and allspice, stir into cooked apples. Sprinkle extra cinnamon over bottom of mold. Quickly dip one circle of bread into melted butter and fit into bottom of charlotte mold. In the same manner, dip the bread fingers and stand up around the inside of mold, overlapping one another. Fill with apple slices. Cover with second bread circle, also dipped in butter.

Mix the topping of sugar and spices, sprinkle over bread. Add one-quarter cup water and cover with foil. Bake 25-30 minutes. Allow to cool 10 minutes in pan, then invert on a platter. Serve with vanilla or ginger ice cream or whipped cream.

SERVES 4.

Pommes charlotte is the French version of the Amish specialty apple pandowdy. For authenticity bake in a charlotte mold.

## PUFFED APPLE PANCAKE

1¼   cups sifted flour
2    tablespoons sugar
½    teaspoon salt
½    teaspoon cinnamon
6    eggs, beaten
1½   cups milk
½    teaspoon vanilla
½    cup butter or margarine
4    apples, peeled and sliced
     cinnamon
     brown sugar

Preheat oven to 425 degrees. Combine flour, sugar, salt, and cinnamon in large bowl. Add eggs, milk, and vanilla. Beat until batter is smooth. Melt butter in oven in 9 x 13-inch pan. Add apples and sprinkle with cinnamon and brown sugar. Allow to sizzle in butter a few minutes, but do not let butter brown. Pour batter over apples, sprinkle with brown sugar and bake about 15 minutes. Reduce heat to 350 degrees and finish cooking another 5-10 minutes.

SERVES 4-6.

**This German-style puffed pancake will delight all your guests. Accompany with ham or Canadian bacon slices.**

## POACHED PEARS
## WITH BLACKBERRY WINE SORBET

2    ripe Bartlett pears
1    bottle late harvest Riesling wine
3    fresh basil leaves
2    cups Michigan blackberry wine
     GARNISH:
     fresh berries or fresh basil leaves

Peel pears, cut in half, and scoop out core with a small spoon. Heat Riesling wine with basil leaves in a heavy saucepan. Bring to a boil, reduce to a simmer, add pears, and poach until tender. Remove pears with a slotted spoon, cool, and refrigerate. Strain wine and bring back to a boil. Reduce to 1 cup and chill. Add 2 cups blackberry wine to saucepan and reduce by half. Pour into metal bowl and place in freezer, stirring every 30 minutes for 3 hours. Cover and freeze 1 additional hour. To serve, pour a small pool of reduced Riesling onto individual plates or serving platter. Arrange pears on liquid, scoop out blackberry wine sorbet next to each pear, and garnish plate with fresh berries or a sprig of fresh basil leaves. Serve immediately.

SERVES 4.

**Meadowbrook Hall
Rochester, Michigan**

## RHUBARB COFFEE CAKE

½ cup butter or margarine, softened
1½ cups sugar
1 egg
1 cup buttermilk
1 teaspoon baking soda
1 teaspoon vanilla
½ teaspoon salt
2½ cups flour
3 cups sliced rhubarb
1 cup light brown sugar
½ cup chopped walnuts
TOPPING:
½ cup butter
1 cup sugar
½ cup light cream
1 teaspoon vanilla

Preheat oven to 350 degrees. In a mixer bowl, blend together butter, sugar, egg, buttermilk, baking soda, vanilla, and salt. Gradually stir in flour. Fold in sliced rhubarb. Grease a 9 x 13-inch baking pan, pour in batter and sprinkle top with brown sugar and nuts. Bake for 45 minutes. To prepare topping, mix together butter, sugar, cream, and vanilla in a small saucepan. Stir over medium heat until sugar is dissolved. When cake is done, remove from oven, pierce top with fork, then slowly pour topping over cake allowing it to soak in. Cool in pan on wire rack before cutting and serving.

SERVES 16-20.

**Although the rhubarb season is a short one, unsweetened frozen rhubarb makes a suitable substitute all year round.**

## PECAN ROLLS

1 cup melted shortening or butter
1¼ cups milk
1 cup sugar
1 teaspoon salt
½ ounce (2 scant tablespoons) dry yeast
¼ cup warm water
6-7 cups flour
4 eggs beaten
1¼ cups melted butter, divided
¾ cup sugar
2 teaspoons cinnamon
1½ cups brown sugar
2 cups pecan halves

Combine shortening, milk, sugar, and salt. Set aside. Soften yeast in water. Combine yeast mixture with milk mixture. Add half the flour and the eggs. Beat well. Add remaining flour. Knead for 10 minutes. Place in a large well-greased bowl, turn over and cover with waxed paper and a kitchen towel. Let rise until doubled, approximately 3 hours. On a large floured board, roll out dough one-half inch thick, brush with one-half cup melted butter. Mix sugar and cinnamon and sprinkle over buttered dough. Roll up jelly roll style. Cut rolls 1 inch thick. To cut without mashing the dough, slide a thread under the roll, bring ends up over roll, cross and pull. Divide the melted butter and brown sugar equally into 3 cake pans, 8 x 8 inches. Press pecans face down in brown sugar. Place 8 rolls per pan, cut side down, on top, arranging small roll in the center. Cover and let rise until doubled. Preheat oven to 375 degrees. Bake 25 minutes or until light brown. To freeze, wrap whole cake in foil. Reheat a few minutes and pull apart before serving.

SERVES 24.

A bee is buzzing in my bonnet—

I'd rather have him buzzing on it!

# HERBS
# &
# SPICES

## Provençal Herb Mix and Dressing

HERB MIX:

1 tablespoon dried parsley
1 tablespoon dried chervil
½ teaspoon dried rosemary
1 finely crumbled bay leaf
¼ teaspoon crushed fennel seeds
PROVENÇAL DRESSING:
1 cup mayonnaise
½ cup plain yogurt
2 tablespoons Provençal herb mix
1 tablespoon dry Madeira
salt and freshly ground black pepper to taste

Mix the herbs, bay leaf, and fennel seeds together and store in a tightly sealed jar.

To prepare dressing: Combine mayonnaise, yogurt, herb mix, and wine in a bowl or a blender. Blend or whisk together. Season with salt and pepper. Refrigerate 2 hours before using.

MAKES 1½ CUPS DRESSING.

**Sprinkle herb mix over sole or salmon filets before baking; add to a basic vinaigrette; or use in zesty Provençal dressings, excellent over salad greens or tossed with fresh steamed vegetables, served hot or cold.**

## Herb Society Butter

½ cup unsalted butter, softened
½ teaspoon dried basil
½ teaspoon dried chervil
½ teaspoon dried parsley
½ teaspoon dried chives
1 teaspoon grated lemon zest

Mix softened butter, herbs, and lemon zest together with a spoon or mixer. Spoon into a small crock or butter mold. Decorate top with a fresh Italian parsley leaf or by scoring with the tines of a fork. Cover and refrigerate at least 2 hours before using. (Note: To substitute fresh herbs for dried, mince very finely, using twice the amount.)

MAKES ½ CUP.

**The Southern Michigan Herb Society created this favorite herb butter. Prepare a few hours before using so that the flavors can blend thoroughly.**

## SAVORY HERB BUTTER

½  cup unsalted butter, softened
½  teaspoon dried basil
½  teaspoon dried oregano
½  teaspoon dried lemon balm leaves
½  teaspoon dried dill leaves

Mix softened butter and herbs together with a spoon or mixer. Spoon into a small serving crock or butter mold. Cover and refrigerate at least 2 hours before using.

MAKES ½ CUP.

**These savory herbal flavors blend well with fish and poultry or tossed into freshly cooked pasta noodles.**

## SALLY'S HERB BUTTER

½  cup unsalted butter or unsalted margarine
⅛  teaspoon lemon juice
½  teaspoon dried basil
¼  teaspoon dried marjoram
¼  teaspoon dried savory

Cream butter, add lemon juice and herbs. Mix well. Spoon into small serving crock. Cover and refrigerate at least 2 hours before using.

MAKES ½ CUP.

**This herbal combination harmonizes with beef, poultry, vegetables, and legumes.**

## Violets in May Salad

¾   cup virgin olive oil
3-4   tablespoons wine vinegar to taste
1½   teaspoons salt, rubbed with 1 peeled garlic clove
1   teaspoon ground black pepper
6   large heads Bibb lettuce, rinsed, torn, ribs removed
1   pound fresh mushrooms, sliced horizontally
2   cups sliced cooked beets
1   bouquet fresh violets (about 3 dozen)

In a bowl, jar, or blender, mix together oil, vinegar, salt and pepper. Set dressing aside. Toss together broken lettuce pieces, mushroom slices, and beets. Add enough dressing to moisten salad. Trim stems from violets and arrange blossoms artistically over salad.

SERVES 8-10.

**Pick violets just before tossing salad, or store them in the refrigerator in a glass of water. You may substitute Johnny-Jump-Ups or other edible flowers when violets are no longer in bloom.**

## Ensalada de Capuchinas (Nasturtium Salad)

2-3   tablespoons red wine or raspberry vinegar, or to taste
½   cup olive oil
1   tablespoon Dijon mustard
¼   teaspoon salt
¼   cup fresh tarragon leaves (or 2 tablespoons dried, crumbled)
   ground black pepper to taste
2   heads leaf lettuce, rinsed, torn, ribs removed
¼   pound very thinly sliced cucumbers
16   nasturtiums, blossoms only
   GARNISH:
8-10   Belgian endive spears

In a jar, bowl, or blender, mix together vinegar, oil, mustard, salt, and tarragon. Season with black pepper. Set dressing aside. In a salad bowl, toss together lettuce pieces and cucumber slices with enough dressing to moisten. Sprinkle blossoms over top. Arrange endive pieces vertically around inside of bowl.

SERVES 8.

**This summer salad nearly glows with the glorious colors of red, orange, and yellow nasturtiums.**

## Springtime Herb Potato Salad

2 pounds small new potatoes, unpeeled
½ cup dry white wine
2 tablespoons chopped fresh parsley
2 tablespoons chopped fresh chives
1 tablespoon chopped sweet woodruff
   or fresh chervil
2 tablespoons finely minced shallots or red onions
½ cup olive oil
2½ tablespoons white wine or champagne vinegar
1 rounded teaspoon French style mustard
   salt and freshly ground pepper

In a large saucepan, bring potatoes to a boil. Reduce temperature and simmer 10-15 minutes until tender. Drain water and cut potatoes in half. Combine wine, herbs, and shallots and pour over hot potatoes. When potatoes are completely cool, drain off any wine that has not been absorbed. Mix together olive oil, vinegar, mustard, salt, and pepper. Pour over potatoes and toss gently. Serve at room temperature.

SERVES 6-8.

## Marinated Tomatoes

¼ cup olive oil
2 tablespoons tarragon or cider vinegar
2 teaspoons mustard
⅓ cup chopped parsley
1 clove garlic, crushed
1 teaspoon sugar
½ teaspoon salt
¼ teaspoon pepper
6-8 ripe tomatoes

Combine all ingredients except tomatoes in a jar. Cover and shake well. Set marinade aside. Peel tomatoes and, if necessary, cut a thin slice from the bottoms so tomatoes sit flat. Slice tomatoes crosswise into even slices, and restack into tomato shapes. Place in container large enough to hold the stacks side by side. Pour marinade over the tomatoes, cover container, and put in refrigerator for 1-2 hours. Spoon marinade over tomato stacks several times. Remove from refrigerator one-half hour before serving. Lift out tomato stacks, and serve on lettuce leaves.

SERVES 6-8.

## Garlic-Herb Salt

2¼   *teaspoons paprika*
½   *teaspoon thyme*
½   *teaspoon marjoram*
¼   *teaspoon garlic powder*
⅛   *teaspoon onion powder*
⅛   *teaspoon dill*
3   *tablespoons salt substitute*

 Mix together herbs, spices, and salt substitute in a small glass jar. Seal tightly. Shake well before using. Store in a cool, dry place.

For those who must limit salt in their diet, this sodium-free mix adds lots of flavor to salad dressing, broiled fish, or even hamburger.

## Herb Toast

½   *pound butter or margarine*
2   *tablespoons toasted sesame seeds*
1   *tablespoon chopped chives*
2   *tablespoons chopped parsley*
1   *teaspoon tarragon*
1   *teaspoon marjoram*
   *thin sliced bread*

 Preheat oven to 300 degrees. Mix together butter, seeds, and herbs. Cut bread slices in half diagonally and spread with butter mixture. Bake for 20 minutes or until dry.

An interesting alternative to quick breads and delightful when served with scrambled eggs or an omelet.

## YORKSHIRE WINE MARINADE

¼ teaspoon dried marjoram
¼ teaspoon dried thyme
4 whole black peppercorns
1 teaspoon allspice berries
3-4 whole cloves
1 carrot, diced
1 large onion, diced
1 tablespoon dried parsley
  (or 2 tablespoons fresh)
1½ cups red wine
½ cup virgin olive oil
2 tablespoons wine vinegar
1 lemon, sliced

 Mix all ingredients together except for the lemon. Use to marinate meat or fish, topped with lemon slices, for 2 hours. Refrigerate.

MAKES 2 CUPS, ENOUGH FOR 2 POUNDS OF MEAT.

This herb and spice blend works especially well for grilled beef and lamb. For fish, substitute white wine for the red.

## LAVENDER VINEGAR

1 pint cider vinegar
¼ cup lavender heads

 Cold method: Mix together in a glass jar or bottle. Seal and allow to set 2-6 weeks before using. Heat method: Heat the vinegar just until it begins to steam. Pour hot vinegar over lavender blossom heads in a glass jar or bottle and seal. Allow to set 3 days before using.

MAKES 1 PINT.

Use either in a salad dressing or as a bath or facial astringent. Recipe requires from several days to several weeks aging, depending on the method used.

## Aromatic Olive Oil

3  small sprigs fresh oregano
3  small sprigs fresh thyme
1  garlic clove, peeled
1  pint extra virgin olive oil

 Gently heat oil until warm and fragrant. Pour heated oil into a 1-pint glass jar or bottle containing fresh herbs and garlic. Allow to cool and cover tightly. Keep stored 2 weeks before using.

MAKES 1 PINT.

**Flavored olive oils add an extra dimension to a home-made salad dressing or when sautéing veal scallops or chicken. Substitute chervil, tarragon, and shallots in combination for variety.**

## Quick Pesto

2  cups fresh basil leaves, stems removed
½  cup fresh parsley leaves, stems removed
2  garlic cloves, peeled
1  teaspoon salt
½  cup freshly grated Parmesan cheese
¼  cup pine nuts
½  cup olive oil plus additional for sealing

 Purée basil leaves, parsley leaves, garlic cloves, and salt in a blender. Add Parmesan cheese and pine nuts. Purée until smooth and thick. Slowly add olive oil. Stop and stir twice. Continue to purée until the consistency is that of a creamed butter. Spoon into a glass jar with lid, add a thin layer of olive oil to help keep pesto fresh, cover tightly. Store in the refrigerator up to 2 weeks.

MAKES ABOUT 1½ CUPS.

**A tablespoon or two of pesto adds zip to a pot of mine-strone soup. Toss into freshly made pasta or add a teaspoon to a cup of a homemade vinaigrette.**

## GARLIC HERB SAUCE

1    *large garlic clove, finely minced*
¾   *cup plain yogurt*
2    *tablespoons mixed fresh herbs, parsley, dill,*
      *tarragon, and chives (or 1 tablespoon dried)*
      *dash of salt*
      *freshly ground black pepper to taste*

In a bowl or blender, mix together garlic, yogurt, herbs, and seasonings. Refrigerate 3-4 hours before using.

MAKES ¾ CUP.

A low-calorie, low-salt vegetable dip. Also use to accompany fish, poultry, lamb, or on a baked potato.

## GREEN MAYONNAISE SAUCE

⅔   *cup prepared light mayonnaise*
⅓   *cup plain low-fat yogurt*
1    *tablespoon lemon juice*
2    *tablespoons half & half*
      *salt to taste*
2    *tablespoons fresh minced lovage or Italian*
      *parsley*

Mix ingredients in food processor or blender. Put in glass bowl or jar, cover and refrigerate. Serve on sliced tomatoes, as a dip for raw vegetables, or as salad dressing.

MAKES ABOUT 1 CUP.

Lovage is a hardy perennial, with a celery-like flavor. Its fresh leaves are superb when finely minced and added to a green salad.

## Herbed Honey Mustard

¾   *cup Dijon mustard*
½   *cup plus 1 tablespoon sour cream*
4   *rounded tablespoons honey*
1   *teaspoon dried tarragon*
1   *teaspoon dried basil leaves*
¼   *teaspoon dried thyme*
¼   *teaspoon crushed fennel seeds*
¼   *teaspoon crushed, dried lavender blossoms*
    *(optional)*

 In a 1-quart bowl, whisk together the mustard, sour cream, and honey. Add dried herbs and whisk until blended. Cover and refrigerate 2 hours before serving. Keep refrigerated up to 1 month.

MAKES 1½ CUPS.

## Sweet Lemon Bar-B-Que

¾   *cup honey*
½   *cup fresh lemon juice*
1   *teaspoon oregano*
1   *teaspoon dill*

 Beat together honey and lemon juice with a wire whisk. Add oregano and dill. Mix well. Use as you would any barbeque sauce. Works well on skinned chicken breasts.

MAKES 1¼ CUPS.

**Great for grilling chicken on a picnic!**

## LAVENDER WHIPPED CREAM

1 cup heavy cream
3 tablespoons fresh lavender flowers, stems removed (or 1 tablespoon dried)
1 tablespoon sugar

 In a small bowl, combine cream and fresh lavender. Cover and refrigerate at least 8 hours, so cream absorbs flavor of flowers. Pour through wire mesh strainer carefully to remove lavender. Beat cream until almost stiff, then gradually add sugar. Continue to beat until stiff peaks form. Sprinkle a few lavender flowers over the cream before serving.

MAKES 2 CUPS.

**A bit of Victorian days-gone-by, comes to a summer porch party or an English tea. Serve this lavender scented cream with pound cake, or chiffon or angel food cake, set on a paper lace doily surrounded by lavender flower heads. It also complements fresh fruit.**

## ORANGE BASIL COOKIES

⅓ cup butter
9 ounces cream cheese
1 egg yolk
1 tablespoon orange juice
1 orange cake mix (1 pound 2 ounces)
1 teaspoon grated orange zest
1 cup raisins
½ cup chopped walnuts
2 tablespoons dried basil

 Mix together butter, cream cheese, egg yolk, and orange juice. Add dry cake mix. Stir in orange zest, raisins, walnuts, and basil. Chill dough. Preheat oven to 350 degrees. Roll chilled dough into half-inch balls and place on buttered cookie sheets. Flatten each ball with a fork. Bake for 10-15 minutes. (Variation: Lemon cake mix and 1 tablespoon frozen orange juice concentrate can be substituted for orange cake mix and 1 tablespoon orange juice.) For a bit of artistry, attach a small paper or silk leaf using a dab of confectioners' sugar icing.

MAKES 6-7 DOZEN.

**This unusual combination of flavors always brings rave reviews.**

## ROSE GERANIUM SYRUP

## CRYSTALLIZED FLOWERS

*1   cup sugar*
*1   cup water*
*2   peppermint scented geranium leaves*
*3   rose scented geranium leaves*

*edible flowers or herbs, fresh, dry, insect-free*
*egg whites*
*superfine granulated sugar*

 Combine the sugar and water in a small saucepan. Cook over medium heat. Stir until sugar dissolves. Bring mixture to a boil and reduce temperature to a simmer. Remove from heat when liquid reaches a syrup consistency. Add geranium leaves. Cover and let stand until syrup reaches room temperature. Refrigerate overnight. Remove leaves before serving. Store in a glass jar or bottle with a tight-fitting lid.

 Gently rinse off blossoms, allow to dry thoroughly. Beat egg whites lightly. Using a small paint brush, coat petals with egg whites. Sprinkle with sugar or gently dip flower to coat. Set on a plate to dry completely. When dry, store in a tightly sealed container.

**This Victorian recipe uses the leaves of rose scented geranium plants. This syrup is excellent drizzled over ice cream, tea cake, or fresh fruit. The recipe may be varied by substituting other combinations of scented geranium leaves, such as orange and almond, apple spice and cinnamon, strawberry and old-fashioned rose, or ginger and orange.**

**Crystal delights of violets, rose petals, lavender, and lilacs provide beautiful decorations for cakes, ice cream, puddings, and salads. Other edible flowers to choose from include: cosmos, nasturtiums, pansies, chive blossoms, fushia, carnations, pinks, and most herbs, such as mint leaves, borage, bee balm, etc.**

Is a good rhyme worth just a dime,

Or maybe a couple of nickels?

But you'll agree its sweeter to me

Than even a couple of pickles.

# CULINARY GIFTS

## Holiday Simmering Spices

2  ounces whole allspice berries
2  ounces whole star anise
2  ounces cinnamon sticks, splintered
2  ounces whole cloves
2  ounces whole ginger, chopped
2  ounces whole nutmeg, crushed
1  ounce orange peel, chopped
6  bay leaves, crushed

To crush cinnamon sticks and nutmeg, set a few at a time on a cloth towel, fold over, and crush with a rubber mallet or rolling pin. Toss all spices together. If used as a gift, wrap in a small cellophane bag and tie with decorative ribbon. Attach a small card listing simmering instructions: Use one pint of water and one tablespoon of mix, simmer on stove for aroma. Do not let mixture boil dry; add water as needed.

**An old-fashioned way to add fragrance to your home. This is a popular item at the Cranbrook Auxiliary fall plant sale, along with Tussy Mussy and Lone Pine Trail potpourris.**

## Shakespeare Potpourri

6  cups mixed flower blossoms, dried (may include carnation, rose, lavender, delphinium, geranium, dahlia, violet, etc. in any pleasing color combination)
1  cup white blossoms, dried (feverfew, baby's breath, achillea the pearl)
4  tablespoons carnation oil
2  tablespoons lavender oil
2  tablespoons powdered orris root

Combine blossoms in a 6-quart kettle. In a small bowl mix together oils and orris root. Add oil mixture to flower petals and blend thoroughly. Store tightly covered. (Note: When working with floral petals and blossoms, dry completely before mixing into potpourri.)

**A beautiful floral variety of color and texture with a hint of carnation fragrance.**

## LONE PINE TRAIL POTPOURRI

2   *cups green cedar fans, clipped fine*
2   *cups juniper greens, no stems, clipped*
2   *cups balsam pine needles*
2   *cups boxwood leaves*
½   *cup tiny hemlock cones*
½   *cup orange peel, diced ½ inch*
½   *cup juniper berries*
5   *tablespoons Christmas pine oil*
2   *tablespoons orris root powder*

In a 6-quart kettle or bowl, combine predried greens, cones, orange peel, and berries. In a small bowl mix pine oil and orris root powder. Stir into potpourri, blending thoroughly. Store in a tightly sealed jar or heavy cellophane bag.

**This evergreen blend is reminiscent of the fresh aroma along the wooded trails which surround Cranbrook House and Gardens.**

## TUSSY MUSSY POTPOURRI

2   *cups dried rose petals*
2   *cups dried French superior blue lavender*
½   *cup dried lamb's ear, center leaves, crumbled*
½   *cup stripped artemesia Silver King*
1   *tablespoon whole cloves*
2   *teaspoons rose geranium oil*
1   *tablespoon rose oil*
2   *teaspoons lavender oil*
2   *teaspoons clove oil*
½   *teaspoon spearmint oil*
2   *tablespoons orris root powder*

In a 6-quart kettle or bowl combine flowers, leaves, and cloves. Mix oils and orris powder in a small bowl. Add oil blend to flower mixture. Stir well to incorporate oil onto each petal. Rub inside of oil bowl thoroughly with dried petals to absorb all the fragrance. Store tightly covered.

**Inspired by a favorite nosegay, Michigan herbalist Caroline Jamison created this floral-spice blend in pastel and silver colors.**

## RASPBERRY CHAMPAGNE VINEGAR

1  heaping quart washed raspberries
2  quarts champagne vinegar
9  tablespoons sugar

 Chop raspberries using food processor. Put in large glass jar (3-4 quart capacity). Stir in 2 quarts champagne vinegar. Keep covered in a cool place. Stir every other day for one month, then strain through several layers of cheesecloth or a fine wire mesh strainer into a large ceramic or stainless steel pot. Add sugar and boil for 5 minutes. Cool slightly. Ladle into sterilized glass jars or decorative small bottles, pouring through cheesecloth-covered funnel. Seal with corks or caps to fit bottles. Refrigerate until used.

MAKES 1-1½ QUARTS.

This is a rich vinegar. Once you've tried it, you'll make it every season!

## HERBED SHERRY

1  bottle (25 ounces) dry sherry, Amontillado or Manzanilla
½  teaspoon dried rosemary
1  sprig thyme
½  teaspoon dried savory
5  black peppercorns
1  teaspoon fennel seeds

 Very gently heat sherry until lukewarm. Be careful not to cook off the alcohol. Add herbs. Pour into large glass jar or original sherry bottle. Allow to sit 2-3 weeks. Strain before using or before pouring into clear decorative glass bottles for gift-giving.

MAKES 1½ PINTS.

A wonderful way to add herb flavoring when deglazing a sauté pan or basting a bird or roast. When giving as a gift, attach a small card listing ingredients and suggestions for ways to use.

## NINE BEAN SOUP

¼  cup dried green split peas
¼  cup dried yellow split peas
¼  cup dried lentils
¼  cup barley
¼  cup dried navy beans
¼  cup dried black beans
¼  cup dried pinto beans
¼  cup dried pink beans
¼  cup dried black-eyed peas
2  quarts water
2  smoked ham hocks
1  large onion
14  ounces beef bouillon
    juice of ½ lemon
28  ounces canned tomatoes with liquid
2  tablespoons dried herbs (basil, thyme,
    marjoram, and sage)
¼  teaspoon ground allspice
    salt and pepper to taste

   Rinse beans and pour into soup kettle. Add water to cover the beans completely and soak 10-12 hours. Drain beans; add 2 quarts water and ham hocks. Bring to boil and simmer 3 hours. Chop the onion and add to bean soup along with the beef bouillon, lemon juice, tomatoes, herbs, and allspice. Simmer 30 minutes or until tender. Add salt and pepper to taste, if desired.

SERVES 12-16.

**For gift-giving, layer dried beans in an attractive glass jar. Attach the recipe with a ribbon.**

## CRYSTAL CUCUMBERS

4  quarts sliced cucumbers
1  cup salt
1  gallon water
1  tablespoon alum
1  tablespoon ground ginger
   SYRUP:
1  cinnamon stick
1  tablespoon pickling spice
1  tablespoon celery seed
3  cups water
1  quart vinegar
6  cups sugar

In a large bowl or crock, cover cucumbers with salt and water, let stand 8 days. Drain and discard brine. Place cucumbers in large kettle, add water to cover and alum. Bring to a boil, remove from heat, let stand 20 minutes. Drain and discard liquid. Add ginger and water to cover. Bring to boil, remove from heat, let stand 30 minutes. Drain and discard liquid. Tie spices in a cheesecloth bag, add to other syrup ingredients and bring to boil. Add cucumbers and bring to a boil again. Discard spice bag, pack and process 5 minutes.

MAKES 16 HALF-PINT JARS.

**A tangy pickle which almost becomes translucent.**

## RATATOUILLE RELISH

1½  pounds eggplant, pared and chopped
½  pound zucchini, thinly sliced
2  teaspoons pickling salt, divided
1  cup chopped onion
2  cloves garlic, minced
½  cup olive oil
2  green peppers, cut into ¼-inch-wide strips
2  pounds tomatoes, peeled, seeded, and chopped
1  teaspoon dried basil
⅛  teaspoon pepper

Sprinkle eggplant and zucchini with 1 teaspoon salt and let stand 1 hour. Drain and pat dry. Sauté onion and garlic in oil 5 minutes in a large skillet. Add green peppers, tomatoes, eggplant, and zucchini. Heat to boiling. Simmer covered until vegetables are tender, about 30 minutes. Add basil, remaining salt, and pepper. Simmer uncovered for 10 minutes or until thick. Pack in sterilized jars and seal. Process in canning kettle for 10 minutes. Also freezes well.

MAKES 3 PINTS.

**Can be served cold as a relish or heated as a vegetable side dish.**

## CRANBERRY-RASPBERRY RELISH

1  pound fresh cranberries
2  Granny Smith apples, peeled
1  scant cup sugar
10  ounces frozen raspberries, thawed and drained
1  teaspoon lemon juice
½  cup orange marmalade

Evenly chop cranberries and apples by hand or in a food processor (be careful not to liquefy). Combine chopped fruit, sugar, raspberries, and lemon juice in a medium bowl. Toss until well blended. Stir in marmalade. Store covered and refrigerated up to 4 weeks. For gift-giving pack in a decorative glass jar with a tight-fitting lid. Attach a reminder label to keep refrigerated.

MAKES APPROXIMATELY 4 CUPS.

**A colorful gift to take during the winter holidays.**

## PEAR HONEY

## CRANBERRY PORT WINE JELLY

5 pounds fully ripened Bartlett pears
5 cups sugar
¼ cup fresh lemon juice
½ teaspoon cloves
½ teaspoon cinnamon
½ teaspoon nutmeg
6 ounces liquid fruit pectin

7 cups sugar
3 cups cranberry juice
¼ teaspoon ground cinnamon
¼ teaspoon ground cloves
1 cup good port wine
6 ounces liquid pectin

 Peel, seed, and core ripe pears. Finely chop, but do not liquefy, in a food processor or with a chef's knife. Mix pears, sugar, lemon juice, and spices together in a large pot. Bring ingredients to a boil, then reduce temperature and simmer 30 minutes, stirring frequently. Remove from heat, add pectin, and pour into hot, sterilized 8-ounce jars. Seal with paraffin.

MAKES 8 JARS, 8 OUNCES EACH.

 Combine sugar, cranberry juice, ground cinnamon, and ground cloves in a heavy, large saucepan. Bring to a boil, stirring frequently. Remove from heat; stir in wine and pectin. Skim off foam with a metal spoon. Quickly pour jelly into hot sterilized jars, leaving a half-inch headspace. Seal at once with a thin layer of paraffin. Cover with lids.

MAKES 9 HALF-PINT JARS.

**Although honey is not among the ingredients in this fruit spread, this old Quaker recipe has the consistency of honey. Serve on hot biscuits, toast, and muffins.**

**This is one jelly which can be made year round. It's ruby color makes it a pretty gift appropriate for all the winter holidays.**

## CRANBERRY PEACH CHUTNEY

1   onion, minced
1   clove garlic, minced
1   cup golden raisins
4   cups fresh cranberries
4   cups diced canned peaches, drained
1   tablespoon chili powder
½   cup chopped crystallized ginger
½   cup chopped nuts
2   tablespoons mustard seed
1   tablespoon salt
4   cups cider vinegar
2   cups firmly packed light brown sugar

Combine all ingredients in a soup pot. Bring to a boil, then simmer, uncovered, for 2 hours or until mixture is thick. Stir occasionally to prevent sticking. Spoon mixture into sterilized jars, seal and cool.

MAKES 3-4 PINTS.

## PEAR CHUTNEY

4½   pounds firm, ripe Bartlett pears, peeled, cored, and chopped (approximately 8 cups)
2½   cups light brown sugar
2     cups white vinegar
1½   cups golden or dark raisins
½     cup chopped onion
½     cup chopped crystallized ginger
2     tablespoons mustard seed, crushed in a mortar
1     tablespoon salt
3     cloves garlic, minced
½     teaspoon ground red pepper

Combine all ingredients in a large saucepan. Bring to a boil over medium heat, stirring frequently. Reduce heat to simmer and cook until thick, about 40-60 minutes, stirring occasionally. Pour chutney into hot, sterilized, half-pint jars. Wipe rims clean and tightly seal lids. Arrange jars in a large pot and cover by 1 inch with boiling water. Cover pot and boil for 10 minutes. Remove jars from water bath and cool. Store sealed jars in a cool, dry place. (If lid pops up when pressed, store chutney in refrigerator.)

MAKES 8 HALF-PINT JARS.

**Pear chutney complements pork dishes as well as poultry and lamb.**

## OLD-FASHIONED RASPBERRY JAM

4   *heaping cups raspberries*
4   *scant cups sugar*
1   *tablespoon epsom salts*

 In a heavy saucepan, mix together raspberries and sugar. Boil 5 minutes, stirring occasionally (burns easily). Remove from heat, add epsom salts and stir constantly for 5 minutes. Pour into sterilized jars and seal with paraffin.

MAKES 5 HALF-PINT JARS.

**This tried-and-true jam technique works wonderfully. You'll never use pectin again.**

## PEACH AND GINGER JAM

6   *cups sugar*
3½ *pounds fully ripe peaches*
    *(5 cups finely chopped)*
⅓  *cup finely slivered crystallized ginger*
1¾ *ounces powdered fruit pectin*

 Measure sugar into a large, heavy saucepan. Peel peaches; in a food processor, grind or chop very fine. Measure 5 cups of fruit into saucepan. Add ginger and fruit pectin, mixing well. Bring mixture to a full rolling boil; boil hard 1 minute, stirring constantly. Remove from heat and skim off foam with a metal spoon. Stir and skim for 5 minutes to cool slightly and prevent floating fruit. Ladle quickly into hot, sterilized jars. Seal at once with thin layer of hot paraffin. Cover with lids.

MAKES 8-9 HALF-PINT JARS.

**A zesty jam which nicely complements scones or biscuits.**

## Vin D'Orange à la Maison

1    *pound granulated or superfine cane sugar*
1    *pint brandy*
3    *bottles dry white wine*
½    *teaspoon orange blossom water*
6    *cloves*
3    *cinnamon sticks, 3-4 inches long*
2    *star anise*
2    *oranges, quartered and seeded*
     *vanilla bean, 3-inch piece*

 In a large pot or mixing bowl, dissolve sugar in brandy. Add wine and orange blossom water. When thoroughly mixed, pour into a sterilized half-gallon container with a tight-fitting lid. Pack the jar with orange quarters, cloves and anise. Crack the cinnamon sticks and vanilla bean with your fist to release their flavor and add to jar. Cover tightly and store in a cool, dark place for 5-6 weeks. Strain and pour into sterilized wine bottles.

MAKES 4 BOTTLES, 750 ML. EACH.

**A French orange dessert wine which is traditionally served on Christmas Eve with the Thirteen Desserts of Christmas throughout Provence.**

## French Preserved Raspberries and Liqueur

4    *cups fresh unblemished raspberries*
18    *ounces good quality brandy*
½    *cup sugar or superfine sugar*
½    *cup crème de cassis liqueur*
     *(French black currant liqueur)*

 Use only select raspberries. Rinse carefully and spoon into a sterilized 1-liter glass jar, preferably with a rubber ring and spring lid. In a ceramic bowl, mix sugar and brandy until dissolved. Pour over berries. Add one-half cup liqueur. Cover tightly. Refrigerate 2-3 weeks. To use or give liqueur as a gift, carefully strain into small glass bottles and seal. Store remaining berries in refrigerator, covered with liqueur.

MAKES 1 LITER.

**After preserving, this berry flavored liqueur can be given as a gift or kept to preserve the raspberries for year-long use in desserts, sauces, or as a garnish.**

## CÔTE BASQUE COFFEE

¼  pound French roast whole coffee beans
¾  pound Hawaiian Kona whole coffee beans
½  cup toasted slivered almonds
2  cinnamon sticks (3-4 inches long), crushed
¼  teaspoon anise seeds
1  vanilla bean (3-4 inches long)

 Mix the coffee beans together in a large bowl. Add toasted almonds, cinnamon, and anise seeds. Mix well. Pack into a 1-quart glass or porcelain jar with a tight-fitting lid. Set vanilla bean in center. Seal. Allow flavors to blend 5-6 days before using. To prepare for brewing, grind coffee beans with toasted almonds and anise seeds only. Store up to 1 month.

MAKES 1 POUND.

**Whole coffee beans make an attractive gift when packed in a clear glass, spring-loaded jar. Tie a colorful ribbon around the neck of the jar and attach a decorative coffee measure. You may wish to add recipe instructions on a small tag.**

## BUCKEYES

1  pound confectioners' sugar
½  cup butter or margarine, softened
1½  cups creamy peanut butter
1  teaspoon vanilla
6  ounces chocolate chips
1  tablespoon vegetable oil

 In a large electric mixer bowl, blend together sugar, butter, and peanut butter. Add vanilla and stir. Cover and refrigerate 3-4 hours. Shape dough into 60 balls (approximately 1-inch diameter). Refrigerate. Line a cookie sheet with waxed paper. In a double boiler melt chocolate and oil. Using a toothpick, quickly dip chilled balls into melted chocolate to coat all but a small spot on each cookie. Set on wax paper and refrigerate or freeze until chocolate is firm. Gift pack in decorative boxes or tins for football fans and peanut butter aficionados.

5 DOZEN.

**Michiganians consider eating Buckeyes for dessert an essential part of any Michigan-Ohio State tailgate party.**

## Black Walnut Fudge

2 ounces unsweetened chocolate
4 cups sugar
1½ cups coffee cream or light cream
½ teaspoon salt
1 cup white corn syrup
1 teaspoon vanilla
½ cup black or English walnuts, finely chopped

 In a heavy saucepan, melt chocolate. Add sugar, cream, salt, and corn syrup. Cook to 240 degrees, just above soft-ball stage. Add vanilla. Let cool, then beat until creamy and mixture loses its shine. Fold in nuts. Pour into a buttered 8 x 8-inch pan. Allow to set overnight before cutting.

MAKES 3 DOZEN SQUARE PIECES.

Nut fudge makes a delectable old-fashioned gift for teachers, family, and friends, especially when packed in a brightly colored foil-covered box.

## Turtle Bars

2 cups flour
1 cup packed brown sugar
½ cup butter
TOPPING:
1½ cups whole pecans
⅔ cup butter
½ cup brown sugar
12 ounces chocolate chips

 Preheat oven to 350 degrees. With an electric mixer, mix flour, brown sugar, and butter at medium speed 2-3 minutes. Pat firmly in 13 x 9 x 2-inch pan. Sprinkle pecans over unbaked crust. Combine butter and brown sugar and cook over medium heat until mixture comes to a boil. Boil one-half to 1 minute stirring constantly. Pour evenly over pecans. Bake 18-22 minutes or until entire layer is bubbly and crust is a light golden brown. Remove and sprinkle chips over surface. Slightly swirl with the back of a spoon after 2-3 minutes. Cool and cut into bars.

MAKES 3 DOZEN.

This is a wonderful way to enjoy the flavor of a traditional turtle cookie without all the fuss.

## GREEN TREES SUGAR COOKIES

3 cups flour
1 teaspoon baking powder
¼ teaspoon salt
1 teaspoon ground cinnamon
½ teaspoon ground allspice
¾ cup unsalted butter, softened
1 cup sugar
2 eggs, room temperature
1 teaspoon vanilla

DECORATORS' ICING:
1½ cups sifted confectioners' sugar, divided
1½ egg whites, divided
3 teaspoons lemon juice, divided
green food coloring
6 ounces green candy-making chocolate wafers, melted
(available at candy-making supply shops)

In a large bowl, mix together flour, baking powder, salt, and spices. Set aside. In a mixer bowl, beat together butter and sugar until light and fluffy. Add eggs and vanilla, beat again. Carefully fold in the flour mixture, blending just until smooth. Divide dough into quarters and wrap separately in wax paper. Refrigerate 1 hour or until firm. Preheat oven to 375 degrees. Remove one packet of dough at a time and roll on a lightly floured board to one-eighth-inch thickness. Cut with floured cutter and set on greased cookie sheets. Bake for 8-10 minutes until lightly golden. Remove and cool on a rack.

In mixer bowl, blend together 1 cup confectioners' sugar, 1 egg white, and 2 teaspoons lemon juice. Beat until smooth. Add green food coloring, 1 drop at a time, until a pale or medium shade of green is achieved. Set aside. In a separate bowl, mix together remaining one-half cup confectioners' sugar, one-half egg white, and 1 teaspoon lemon juice. Beat until smooth. Set aside. After cookies have cooled, dip the outer branches into the green icing coating one-half of the cookie. Remove excess and set on a rack to dry. When dry, dip green edges into white icing or dab on white icing with a small paint brush. Allow to dry. Pour melted chocolate into a pastry bag fitted with a tip with a very small opening. Drizzle chocolate over each cookie to resemble decorative garlands. Set on a rack until completely hardened before packing into tins or wrapping for gifts.

MAKES ABOUT 4 DOZEN.

This colorful decorated cookie is most attractive when cut with a free-form tree pattern, or a pine tree-shape cookie cutter.

## Sugar Spiced Pecans

1   egg white
2   tablespoons cold water
½   cup sugar
½   teaspoon salt
¼   teaspoon ground cinnamon
¼   teaspoon ground cloves
¼   teaspoon ground allspice
1   pound shelled pecans

Preheat oven to 250 degrees. In a 2-quart mixing bowl, whisk together egg white, cold water, sugar, salt, and spices. Add pecans and stir to coat. Arrange pecans in a single layer on a greased cookie sheet. Bake 1 hour. Remove and loosen nuts immediately. When completely cool, pack in decorative glass jars or tins for gift-giving.

MAKES ABOUT 3½ CUPS.

## Old-Fashioned Cinnamon Ornaments

6    tablespoons thick applesauce
10   tablespoons ground cinnamon
     vegetable oil
     nylon thread

In a small saucepan, warm applesauce. Stir in cinnamon until mixture forms a ball. Lightly coat metal or plastic holiday shaped candy mold with oil. Press mixture firmly into mold, smoothing surface. Remove from mold and set aside. Repeat process. Mixture can also be rolled out on a surface lightly dusted with cinnamon and cut with cookie cutters. Use a toothpick to make a small hole at the top of each ornament for hanging. Arrange ornaments on a cake rack and dry in the oven at lowest setting for 6-8 hours with the oven door ajar. When dry, attach a loop of nylon thread through each hole for hanging. (Note: Ornaments are not edible.)

MAKES 6-8 ORNAMENTS.

A simple way to revive a charming holiday tradition. Children will especially enjoy giving these homemade decorations as gifts.

## Acknowledgments

Original nursery rhymes by Henry Scripps Booth and designs by George Gough Booth used as recipe illuminations are courtesy of the Cranbrook Archives.

The Cookbook Committee is grateful to the following volunteers, friends, and professionals who consulted, gave financial support, contributed or tested recipes, and ultimately helped produce
CRANBROOK REFLECTIONS.

Marge Alpern
Daniel Andersen
Susie Andersen
Edie Anderson
Eleanor Barrett
Roslyn Basherian
Lillian Bauder
Ann Besner
Polly Bidwell
Susan Bodary
Patty Boggs
Martha Bones
Helen Booth
Elaine Borruso
Pat Brooker
Susie Brown
Jean Brudaken
Penney Buhler
Cynthia Burdakin
Rosalie Butzel
Nancy Calkins
Christine Cameron
Barbara Caponigro
Rosemary Cartwright
Pam Chandler
Shirlee Citron
Jane Clark
Mark Coir
Dorothy H. Cottrill
Mary Lou Craig
Cherrill Cregar
Johnye Culler
Tirzah Anne Cunningham
Lilo Dare
Bob Davis
Irene Davis
Nancy Diver
Annelise Douglas
Elaine Drane
Elwin's Tu-Go
Barbara Erb
Dorothy Farmer
Margie Fauver

Barbara A. Field
Marty Figley
Janet Fluehr
Joyce Fox
Virginia B. Fox
Marie Gabriel
Lois Gamble
Nancy L. Geddes
Martha Gelder
Fairlie Glynn
Golden Mushroom
Betsy Goldsmith
Diane and Fred Graczyk
Jeanne Graham
Carla Grava
Elwin Greenwald
Paula Griffis
Elaine Gunderson
Jeanne Hackett
Joyce Hague
Barbara Hall
Carolyn Hall
Delores Hamal
Sharon Hansen
Donna K. Hartwig
Karen Haywood
Janet Hildabrand
Ann Hiner
Janet Hogan
Janet S. Houston
Maureen Hoxie
Emily Hranchook
Ruth Hutchins
Dory Izant
Doris Jeffries
Marty John
Nancy Johnson
Pat Johnson
Marge Johnston
Sue Johnston
Susan Jonientz
Juliette Jonna
Vivian Kalmbach

Marguerite Kaufmann
Jan Kennedy
Wally Klein
Charles Klingensmith
Shirley Klipfel
Betty Kneen
Ruth Knights
Harriette Koeneke
Kay Kreutz
Mary Ann Krygier
The Lark Restaurant
Jim and Mary Lark
Florence M. Leasia
Bernice Lee
Sue Leydorf
Judy Lindstrom
Rita Lindstrom
Barbara Long
Eleanor Luedtke
Steven C. Machlay
Nina Machus
Machus Red Fox
Sandy Mackle
Virginia Mackle
Saida Malarney
Mary Marchand
Margaret B. Marentette
Sharon Martin
John McCally
Katherine McCoy
Jane McKee
Elizabeth W. McLean
Phyllis McLean
Meadowbrook Hall
Merchant of Vino
Patricia Miesel
Beverly Miller
Judith Miller
Helene Mills
Ralph Mize
Sandra Moers
Bernice Muench
Laurie Murray

Julie Nagel
Elaine Nauert
Martha Neumann
Frances Nolte
Beverly Nose
Mary Kay Noteman
Regina O'Donnell
Katie Ogden
Olga Omelianoff
Sylvia Paddy
Shirley Park
Louise Parker
By Parrott
Nancy Peil
Pat Plummer
Susan Polich
Winifred E. Polk
Edmund W. Pratt
Irene Prince
Eva Proudfoot
Diane Rancont
Corajoyce Rauss
Clare B. Redfield
Kirsteen Reeve
Sally Riemenschneider
Jean Riggs
Geri Rinschler
Jerry Risk
Gladys Rodgers
Mary Root
Marcy Rosenau
Judy Rosinack
Betty Ross
Linda Roszak
Eloys Rothwell
Shirley Sarver
Leopold K. Schaeli
Karen Serota
Diane Shane
Patty Shea
Kathy Sheean
Dorothy Shoemaker
Glenda Sinn

Barbara Smith
Southern Michigan Herb Society
Polly Spaulding
Hildegard Stanley
Martha Stewart
Norma Stohler
Christine Storfer
Anne Strauss
Midge Stulberg
Claudia Sullivan
David Taylor
Patty Taylor
Stacey Taylor
Molly Tehoy
Sally Ten Eyck
Carolyn Texley
Anne Thompson
Elaine Thorpe
Betsy Todd
Cheryl Trapp
Betty Trost
Florine Trumbull
Van Dyke Place
Lea Van Renterghem
Marilyn Varbedian
Ludmila Von Taube
Betsy Wagner
Edith Wagner
Emmeline Waldsmith
Mary Ann Wallace
Jackie Walley
Ellen Watt
Connie Weber
Jane Wellman
Joan West
Anne Williams
Joyce M. Wilson
Dottie Withrow
Janet Yalsko
Jane Zich

The yews are *you-who*-ing in the yard —

They are waving in the breeze!

Although the cold wind is blowing hard,

I have never heard them sneeze.

# INDEX

## A

APPETIZERS
CHEESE
  Apricot Brandied Brie 19
  Three-Cheese Torta with Pine Nuts 27
DIPS
  Blue Cheese Salad Dressing 71
  Chancha en Piedra 30
  Curry Cream Dunk 20
  Garlic Herb Sauce 176
  Green Mayonnaise Sauce 176
  Hummus Bi Tahini 24
  Sweet Red Pepper Dip 31
Garlic Roasted Peppers 21
HOT CANAPÉS
  Artichoke Bagel Bites 25
  Bruschetta 19
  Chèvre Pizza, Nina's 28
  Crab Cup Puffs 29
  Green Onion Rye Melts 24
MEAT
  Sweet and Sour Meatballs 22
  Zakopane 26
MUSHROOMS
  Italian Stuffed Mushrooms, Classic 25
  Marinated Mushrooms 20
  Mushroom Logs 27
  Stuffed Michigan Morels 26
  Wild Mushroom Strudel 22
PÂTÉS
  Chicken Liver Almond Pâté 31
  Smoked Trout Pâté 21
SEAFOOD
  Cold Piquant Shrimp 23
  Oysters Rockefeller 30
  Savory Crab Cheese Spread 23
  Shrimp de Jonghe 109
  Smoked Salmon and Wild Mushroom
    Cheesecake 156
  Smoked Salmon Ball 29

APPLES
  Apple-Berry Smoothie 153
  Apple Bread 37
  Apple Cheesecake, Bavarian 142
  Apple-Cherry Toss, Michigan 68
  Apple Tea Punch 153
  Brie and Apples in Puff Pastry 135
  Fresh Apple Nut Cake 143
  Pommes Charlotte 163
  Puffed Apple Pancake 164

Applesauce Date Muffins 36

ARTICHOKES
  Artichoke Hearts Surprise 118
  Phyllo Artichoke Pie 160
  Spinach-Artichoke-Oyster Combo 118

ASPARAGUS
  Chicken and Asparagus Quiche 158
  Fresh Asparagus Salad 70
  Risotto with Asparagus, Tomato, and
    Sage 131
  Vermicelli Noodle Tourte 130

AVOCADOS
  Avocado-Celery Salad 70
  Avocados, Apricots, and Chicken 96

## B

BEEF
  Beef and Mango Curry 76
  Beef-Vegetable Stir-Fry 77
  Brisket, Kansas City 75
  Chili, Danish 77
  Cold Beef Salad Meadowbrook 61
  Creamy Pasta Layers 127
  East Indian Meat Loaf 78
  Lemon Loaves, Six Little 80
  London Broil on the Grill 76
  Picadillo 78
  Steak Soup 57
  Sweet and Sour Meatballs 22
  Tacos, Homestyle 79

BELL PEPPERS
  Chicken Fajitas 96
  Garlic Roasted Peppers 21
  Sweet Red Pepper Dip 31
  Tortilla Medley 117

BERRIES
  Amelanchier Muffins 35
  Berries and Russian Cream 146
  Blueberry Coffee Square 38
  Blueberry Corn Muffins 36
  Cherry Berry Pie, Traverse City 140
  Cranberry Peach Chutney 189
  Cranberry Port Wine Jelly 188
  Cranberry-Raspberry Relish 187
  Preserved Raspberries and Liqueur,
    French 191
  Raspberry Champagne Vinegar 185
  Raspberry Jam, Old-Fashioned 190
  Raspberry Sauce: Chocolate
    Pâté 148
  Raspberry Triangles 145

BEVERAGES
  Apple-Berry Smoothie 153
  Apple Tea Punch 153
  Coffee, Côte Basque 192
  Liqueur, French Preserved
    Raspberries and 191
  Vin D'Orange à la Maison 191

BLUEBERRIES
  see BERRIES

BREADS
  see also COFFEE CAKES;
    MUFFINS; PIZZA
QUICK BREADS
  Apple Bread 37
  Beer Bread, Country 42
  Brown Bread, Potter's 39
  Cheesy Popover Ring 155
  Corn Bread, Village Inn 42
  Drop Biscuits, Americana 41
  Irish Soda Bread 41
  Lemon Nut Bread 38
  Spiced Zucchini Bread 37
  Tea Loaf, English 40
  Tea Scones 40
Stuffing: Roasted Holiday Turkey 97
YEAST BREADS
  Crescent Rolls, Scuppy's 44
  Dilly Cheese Bread 44
  Sweet Bread, Barkas (Czech) 45
  Walnut Raisin Round 39

Broccoli Bake 119
Broccoli Rape, Sautéed, with Fresh Fava
    Beans 117

BUTTERS
    Citrus Butter 162
    Herb Butter, Sally's 170
    Herb Society Butter 169
    Savory Herb Butter 170


# C

CABBAGE
    Freezin' Cole Slaw 69
    Red Cabbage to Blue Kraut 120
    Sweet and Sour Mushrooms and
        Cabbage 122

CAKES
    Black Beast Dessert 147
    Cocoa-Mocha Layer Cake 136
    "Dark Victory" Chocolate Cake 137
    Fresh Apple Nut Cake 143
    "Noir et Blanc" Poppyseed Torte 138

Calzone—"Pizza in a Pocket" 43

CARROTS
    Carrot-Rice Soup with Mango
        Chutney 52
    Carrot-Thyme Soup 54
    Carrots with Lemon and Dill 120
    Potato-Carrot Potage 57

CASSEROLES
    Artichoke Hearts Surprise 118
    Baked Fresh Tomatoes 124
    Broccoli Bake 119
    Cauliflower Medley 121
    Creamy Pasta Layers 127
    Ham Casserole, Country 85
    Marvels of the Sea 111
    Night Before Brunch Bake 159
    Pork Chops, Normandy 86
    Pork Chops, Onions, and Potatoes 87
    Spinach-Artichoke-Oyster Combo 118

Sweet Onion Pudding 122
Sweet Potato Soufflé, Georgian 123
Tomato Pudding Tallyho 125

Cauliflower Medley 121

CHEESE
    Apricot Brandied Brie 19
    Blue Cheese Salad Dressing 71
    Brie and Apples in Puff Pastry 135
    Chèvre Pizza, Nina's 28
    Creamy Pasta Layers 127
    Farmers Cheese Pancakes 154
    Mussel, Spinach, and Brie Soup 53
    Night Before Brunch Bake 159
    Three-Cheese Torta with Pine Nuts 27
    Sunchoke-Leek Soup with Gouda
        Cheese 52

CHEESECAKES
    Apple Cheesecake, Bavarian 142
    Smoked Salmon and Wild Mushroom
        Cheesecake 156

CHERRIES
    Apple-Cherry Toss, Michigan 68
    Cherry Berry Pie, Traverse City 140
    Cherry Cornish Hens Escoffier 98
    Venison Loin with Cherry Sauce 101

CHICKEN
    Apricot Poulet 92
    Avocados, Apricots, and Chicken 96
    Chicken and Asparagus Quiche 158
    Chicken and Tomatoes, Country 91
    Chicken and Wild Rice Salad,
        Anniversary 62
    Chicken Baked with Parmesan 94
    Chicken California Style 95
    Chicken Fajitas 96
    Chicken, Hawaiian Islands 94
    Chicken Liver Almond Pâté 31
    Chicken Pasta Salad, Gatehouse 63
    Chicken Piccata 93
    Chicken Salad, Classic 63
    Curried Chicken Salad 64
    Garlic Chicken, French 91
    Honey Glazed Chicken 93
    Krunchy Ka-Bobs 92

"Paella," Spanish National 106
Stuffed Chicken Breasts,
    Very Italian 95

Chili, Danish 77

CHOCOLATE
    Black Beast Dessert 147
    Black Walnut Fudge 193
    Chocolate Derby Pie 140
    Chocolate Pâté 148
    Choco-Mint Moussecups 146
    Cocoa-Mocha Layer Cake 136
    "Dark Victory" Chocolate Cake 137
    Double Chocolate-Walnut
        Brownies 143
    "Noir et Blanc" Poppyseed Torte 138

CHUTNEYS
    Cranberry Peach Chutney 189
    Pear Chutney 189

COFFEE CAKES
    see also BREADS—Quick Breads
    Blueberry Coffee Square 38
    Coffee Cake Roll, Nana's 45
    Pecan Rolls 165
    Rhubarb Coffee Cake 165

CONDIMENTS
    Cranberry Peach Chutney 189
    Crystal Cucumbers 186
    Garlic-Herb Salt 173
    Herbed Honey Mustard 177
    Pear Chutney 189

COOKIES
BAR COOKIES
    Double Chocolate-Walnut
        Brownies 143
    Pecan Diamonds 144
    Raspberry Triangles 145
    Turtle Bars 193
ROLLED/CUT COOKIES
    Buckeyes 192
    Green Trees Sugar Cookies 194
    Oatmeal Chunkies 145
    Orange Basil Cookies 178
    Patina Di Natale 144

**COOKING WINES, VINEGARS & OILS**
Aromatic Olive Oil 175
Herbed Sherry 185
Lavender Vinegar 174
Raspberry Champagne Vinegar 185

Couscous Salad with Currants and Pine
Nuts 66

**CRAB**
see also SEAFOOD DISHES
Crab Cup Puffs 29
Maryland Crab Cakes 110
Savory Crab Cheese Spread 23

**CRANBERRIES**
see BERRIES

Crystallized Flowers 179

**CUCUMBERS**
Cucumber Soup Emmeline 50
Cucumbers and Cream 121
Crystal Cucumbers 186

**D**

Demi-Glace: Venison Loin with Cherry
Sauce 101

**DESSERTS**
see also CAKES; FROSTINGS,
TOPPINGS &
DECORATIONS; PIES
Apple Cheesecake, Bavarian 142
Berries and Russian Cream 146
Brie and Apples in Puff Pastry 135
Café Cream Toffee Torte 136
Chocolate Pâté 148
Choco-Mint Moussecups 146
Frozen Mocha Mousse 149
Fruit Flan, Company's Coming 149
Poached Pears with Blackberry
Sorbet 164
Pommes Charlotte 163

**E**

**EGG DISHES**
Herb Omelet Torte 157
Night Before Brunch Bake 159

Eggplant, Zucchini, and Mushrooms,
Orecchiette Pasta with 128

**F**

**FILO**
see PHYLLO DISHES

**FISH**
see also SEAFOOD DISHES
Microwave Salmon with Fresh Dill 110
Orange Roughy with Kiwi 113
Pesce Lesso 111
Salad Niçoise 65
Salmon and Lake Trout Medallions
with Sauces "Deux Champagnes"
105
Smoked Salmon and Wild Mushroom
Cheesecake 156
Smoked Salmon Ball 29
Smoked Trout Pâté 21

**FROSTINGS, TOPPINGS &
DECORATIONS**
Carmelized Almonds: Pumpkin
Custard Cream Pie 141
Chocolate Ganache: Black Beast
Dessert 147
Chocolate Ganache: "Dark Victory"
Chocolate Cake 137
Chocolate Ganache: "Noir et Blanc"
Poppyseed Torte 139
Chocolate Leaves: "Noir et Blanc"
Poppyseed Torte 139
Cocoa-Mocha Frosting: Cocoa-Mocha
Layer Cake 136
Crystallized Flowers 179
Custard Sauce: Brie and Apples in
Puff Pastry 135

Lavender Whipped Cream 178
Raspberry Sauce: Chocolate Pâté 148
Rose Geranium Syrup 179

**FRUIT**
see also BERRIES; specific fruits
Blossom Fruit Cup 162
Citrus Butter 162
Fruit Flan, Company's Coming 149
Winter Salad, Bloomfield 67

Fudge, Black Walnut 193

**G**

**GARLIC**
Garlic Chicken, French 91
Garlic-Herb Salt 173

**GIFTS, EDIBLE**
BEVERAGES
Coffee, Côte Basque 192
Vin D'Orange à la Maison 191
CANDIES & NUTS
Black Walnut Fudge 193
Sugar Spiced Pecans 195
CHUTNEYS
Cranberry Peach Chutney 189
Pear Chutney 189
COOKIES
Buckeyes 192
Green Trees Sugar Cookies 194
Turtle Bars 193
COOKING WINES & VINEGARS
Herbed Sherry 185
Raspberry Champagne Vinegar 185
JAMS, JELLIES & SPREADS
Cranberry Port Wine Jelly 188
Peach and Ginger Jam 190
Pear Honey 188
Raspberry Jam, Old-Fashioned 190
Nine Bean Soup 186
PICKLES & RELISHES
Cranberry-Raspberry Relish 187
Crystal Cucumbers 186
Ratatouille Relish 187

Preserved Raspberries and Liqueur,
     French 191

GIFTS, NONEDIBLE
     Cinnamon Ornaments,
          Old-Fashioned 195
     Holiday Simmering Spices 183
     Lone Pine Trail Potpourri 184
     Shakespeare Potpourri 183
     Tussy Mussy Potpourri 184

Gnocchi Verdi 126


# H

HAM
     Baked Ham Loaf with
          Mustard Sauce 160
     Ham Casserole, Country 85

HERB BUTTERS
     see BUTTERS

Herb Mix and Dressing, Provençal 169
Herb Toast 173
Herbed Sherry 185


# J

JAMS, JELLIES & SPREADS
     Cranberry Port Wine Jelly 188
     Peach and Ginger Jam 190
     Pear Honey 188
     Raspberry Jam, Old-Fashioned 190

Jello Salad, Jump for Joy 68


# K

Kiwi, Orange Roughy with 113


# L

LAMB
     Butterflied Leg of Lamb 83
     Minted Lamb Luncheon 83
     Rack of Lamb Ghenghis Khan 84

LEGUMES
     Chili, Danish 77
     Hummus Bi Tahini 24
     Lima Bean Lovers Salad 69
     Navy Bean Soup, Michigan 56
     Nine Bean Soup 186
     Sautéed Broccoli Rape with Fresh
          Fava Beans 117
     Split Pea Soup 56

Lemon Loaves, Six Little 80
Lemon Nut Bread 38


# M

Mango Curry, Beef and 76

MARINADES
     Lamb Marinade: Rack of Lamb
          Ghenghis Khan 84
     Marinade: Marinated Pork Loin 86
     Wine Marinade, Yorkshire 174

MEAT
     see also BEEF; LAMB; PORK;
          VEAL
GAME
     Venison Loin with Cherry Sauce 101
SAUSAGE
     Zakopane 26
     Zucchini Sausage Pie 158

MEAT LOAF
     Baked Ham Loaf with
          Mustard Sauce 160
     Lemon Loaves, Six Little 80
     East Indian Meat Loaf 78


MEATBALLS
     Minted Lamb Luncheon 83
     Sweet and Sour Meatballs 22

MUFFINS
     see also BREADS—Quick Breads
     Amelanchier Muffins 35
     Applesauce Date Muffins 36
     Blueberry Corn Muffins 36
     Mini Spoonfruit Muffins 35

MUSHROOMS
     Marinated Mushrooms 20
     Mushroom Logs 27
     Mushroom Soup, Aunt Jean's
          Polish 54
     Orecchiette Pasta with Eggplant,
          Zucchini, and Mushrooms 128
     Smoked Salmon and Wild Mushroom
          Cheesecake 156
     Stuffed Michigan Morels 26
     Stuffed Mushrooms, Classic Italian 25
     Sweet and Sour Mushrooms and
          Cabbage 122
     Wild Duck with Mushrooms 99
     Wild Mushroom Strudel 22

Mustard, Herbed Honey 177


# N

NUTS
     Black Walnut Fudge 193
     Carmelized Almonds: Pumpkin
          Custard Cream Pie 141
     Couscous Salad with Currants and
          Pine Nuts 66
     Chocolate Derby Pie 140
     Double Chocolate-Walnut
          Brownies 143
     Fresh Apple Nut Cake 143
     Lemon Nut Bread 38
     Pecan Diamonds 144
     Pecan Rolls 165
     Pecan Wild Rice Pilaf 130
     Sugar Spiced Pecans 195

Three-Cheese Torta with Pine Nuts 27
Walnut Raisin Round 39

# O

Oatmeal Chunkies 145
Olive Oil, Aromatic 175

ONIONS
Pork Chops, Onions, and Potatoes 87
Sweet Onion Pudding 122

Ornaments, Old-Fashioned
    Cinnamon 195
Oysters Rockefeller 30

# P

PANCAKES & WAFFLES
Buttermilk Pancakes, The Best 155
Farmers Cheese Pancakes 154
Puffed Apple Pancake 164
Waffles, "No Nothing" 154

PASTA
Chicken Pasta Salad, Gatehouse 63
Creamy Pasta Layers 127
Orecchiette Pasta with Eggplant,
    Zucchini, and Mushrooms 128
Pasta alla Carbonara 129
Pasta with Lemon Cream Sauce 129
Roasted Tomatoes and Onions with
    Spaghetti 127
Seafood Fettucine 113
Stuffed Tomatoes, Patio 125
Vegetable-Fruit Pasta Salad 66
Vermicelli Noodle Tourte 130

PÂTÉS
Chicken Liver Almond Pâté 31
Chocolate Pâté 148
Smoked Trout Pâté 21

PEACHES
Cranberry Peach Chutney 189
Peach and Ginger Jam 190

PEANUT BUTTER
Buckeyes 192
Peanut Butter-Pumpkin Soup 51

PEARS
Pear Chutney 189
Pear Honey 188
Poached Pears with Blackberry Wine
    Sorbet 164

Pesto, Quick 175

PHYLLO DISHES
Phyllo Artichoke Pie 160
Spanakopita (Spinach Pie) 159
Wild Mushroom Strudel 22

PICKLES
Crystal Cucumbers 186

PIES
Cherry Berry Pie, Traverse City 140
Chocolate Derby Pie 140
Puffed Potato Pie 124
Pumpkin Custard Cream Pie 141
Ratatouille Pie 161
Zucchini Sausage Pie 158

PIZZA
Calzone—"Pizza in a Pocket" 43
Chèvre Pizza, Nina's 28

Poppyseed Torte, "Noir et Blanc" 138

PORK
Baked Ham Loaf with
    Mustard Sauce 160
Chinese Spareribs 85
Ham Casserole, Country 85
Marinated Pork Loin 86
Night Before Brunch Bake 159
Pork Chops, Normandy 86
Pork Chops, Onions, and Potatoes 87
Szechwan Pork 87

POTATOES
Herb Potato Salad, Springtime 172
Pork Chops, Onions, and Potatoes 87
Potato-Carrot Potage 57
Puffed Potato Pie 124
Roasted Rosemary Potato Slices 123
Sweet Potato Soufflé, Georgian 123

POTPOURRIS
Holiday Simmering Spices 183
Lone Pine Trail Potpourri 184
Shakespeare Potpourri 183
Tussy Mussy Potpourri 184

POULTRY & GAME BIRDS
    see also CHICKEN
Cherry Cornish Hens Escoffier 98
Curried Duck Salad 99
Roast Pheasant 100
Roasted Holiday Turkey 97
Smothered Quail 98
Wild Duck with Mushrooms 99

PUFF PASTRY DISHES
Brie and Apples in Puff Pastry 135
Herb Omelet Torte 157

PUMPKIN
Peanut Butter-Pumpkin Soup 51
Pumpkin Custard Cream Pie 141

# Q

Quiche, Chicken and Asparagus 158

# R

RASPBERRIES
    see BERRIES

RELISHES
Cranberry-Raspberry Relish 187

Ratatouille Relish 187

**RESTAURANT/PROFESSIONAL RECIPES**
APPETIZERS
  Smoked Salmon and Wild Mushroom
    Cheesecake 156
  Stuffed Michigan Morels 26
  Three-Cheese Torta with Pine Nuts 27
  Wild Mushroom Strudel 22
DESSERTS
  "Dark Victory" Chocolate Cake 137
  "Noir et Blanc" Poppyseed Torte 138
  Poached Pears with Blackberry Wine
    Sorbet 164
FISH & SEAFOOD
  "Paella," Spanish National 106
  Salmon and Lake Trout Medallions
    with Sauces "Deux
    Champagnes" 105
MEAT
  Rack of Lamb Ghenghis Khan 84
  Venison Loin with Cherry
    Sauce 101
POULTRY & GAME BIRDS
  Curried Duck Salad 99
  Roast Pheasant 100
SOUPS
  Mussel, Spinach, and Brie Soup 53
  Tomato-Fennel Soup 49
VEGETABLES, PASTA & RICE
  Autumn Leaves 119
  Risotto with Asparagus, Tomato,
    and Sage 131
  Sautéed Broccoli Rape with Fresh
    Fava Beans 117
  Vermicelli Noodle Tourte 130

Rhubarb Coffee Cake 165

**RICE**
  Chicken and Wild Rice Salad,
    Anniversary 62
  Carrot-Rice Soup with Mango
    Chutney 52
  "Paella," Spanish National 106
  Pecan Wild Rice Pilaf 130
  Rainbow Shrimp Salad 64
  Risotto Parmigiana 131
  Risotto with Asparagus, Tomato, and
    Sage 131

# S

**SALADS**
CHICKEN SALADS
  Chicken and Wild Rice Salad,
    Anniversary 62
  Chicken Pasta Salad, Gatehouse 63
  Chicken Salad, Classic 63
  Curried Chicken Salad 64
Cold Beef Salad Meadowbrook 61
Couscous Salad with Currants and
  Pine Nuts 66
Curried Duck Salad 99
FRUIT SALADS
  Apple-Cherry Toss, Michigan 68
  Avocado-Celery Salad 70
  Vegetable-Fruit Pasta Salad 66
  Winter Salad, Bloomfield 67
Jello Salad, Jump for Joy 68
LETTUCE SALADS
  Caesar Salad, Ross' 65
  Ensalada de Capuchinas (Nasturtium
    Salad) 171
  Violets in May Salad 171
SEAFOOD SALADS
  Rainbow Shrimp Salad 64
  Salad Niçoise 65
VEGETABLE SALADS
  Avocado-Celery Salad 70
  Cucumbers and Cream 121
  Freezin' Cole Slaw 69
  Fresh Asparagus Salad 70
  Herb Potato Salad, Springtime 172
  Lima Bean Lover's Salad 69
  Marinated Tomatoes 172
  Vegetable-Fruit Pasta Salad 66

**SALAD DRESSINGS**
  Blue Cheese Salad Dressing 71
  Celery Seed Salad Dressing 71
  Dressing: Anniversary Chicken and
    Wild Rice Salad 62
  Dressing: Bloomfield Winter Salad 67
  Dressing: Fresh Asparagus Salad 70
  Dressing: Gatehouse Chicken Pasta
    Salad 63
  Dressing, Provençal Herb
    Mix and 169
  Green Mayonnaise Sauce 176

**SAUCES**
  Barbeque Sauce, Aunt Jessie's: Kansas
    City Brisket 75
  Custard Sauce: Brie and Apples in
    Puff Pastry 135
  Garlic Herb Sauce 176
  Green Mayonnaise Sauce 176
  Mustard Sauce, Baked
    Ham Loaf with 160
  Quick Pesto 175
  Sauces "Deux Champagnes,"
    Salmon and Lake Trout
    Medallions with 105
  Sweet Lemon Bar-B-Que 177
  Taco Sauce: Homestyle Tacos 79

**SCALLIONS**
  Cream Olga 55

**SEAFOOD DISHES**
  see also CRAB; FISH; SHRIMP
  Fish Stew Provençal 112
  Marvels of the Sea 111
  Mussel, Spinach, and Brie Soup 53
  Oysters Rockefeller 30
  "Paella," Spanish National 106
  Scallop Chowder, New England 112
  Seafood Fettucine 113
  Spinach-Artichoke-Oyster Combo 118

Sherry, Herbed 185

**SHRIMP**
  see also SEAFOOD DISHES
  Cold Piquant Shrimp 23
  Crackin' Cajun Shrimp 107
  Rainbow Shrimp Salad 64
  Shrimp Bayou 108
  Shrimp de Jonghe 109
  Shrimp Flambé 107
  Shrimp New York, New York 109

Soufflé, Georgian Sweet Potato 123

**SOUPS**
COLD SOUPS
  Carrot-Thyme Soup 54
  Cucumber Soup Emmeline 50
  Garden Vichyssoise 50

Gazpacho, Cranbrook Garden 49
Summer Squash Soup with Fresh
    Herbs 55
HOT SOUPS
    Carrot-Rice Soup with Mango
        Chutney 52
    Carrot-Thyme Soup 54
    Cream Olga 55
    Garden Vichyssoise 50
    Mushroom Soup, Aunt Jean's
        Polish 54
    Mussel, Spinach, and Brie Soup 53
    Navy Bean Soup, Michigan 56
    Nine Bean Soup 186
    Peanut Butter-Pumpkin Soup 51
    Potato-Carrot Potage 57
    Rosemary Autumn Bisque 51
    Scallop Chowder, New England 112
    Split Pea Soup 56
    Steak Soup 57
    Sunchoke-Leek Soup with Gouda
        Cheese 52
    Tomato-Fennel Soup 49

SPINACH
    Gnocchi Verdi 126
    Mussel, Spinach, and Brie Soup 53
    Spanakopita (Spinach Pie) 159
    Spinach-Artichoke-Oyster Combo 118

SQUASH
    Rosemary Autumn Bisque 51
    Summer Squash Soup with Fresh
        Herbs 55

STEWS
    Fish Stew, Provençal 112
    Veal Italiano 81
    Veal Paprikás 81

STIR-FRY
    Beef-Vegetable Stir-Fry 77

Szechwan Pork 87

Stuffing: Roasted Holiday Turkey 97
Sunchoke-Leek Soup with
    Gouda Cheese 52
Sweet Potato Soufflé, Georgian 123
Syrup, Rose Geranium 179

# T

TOAST
    Bruschetta 19
    Herb Toast 173

Tacos, Homestyle 79

TOMATOES
    Baked Fresh Tomatoes 124
    Bruschetta 19
    Chancha en Piedra 30
    Marinated Tomatoes 172
    Roasted Tomatoes and Onions with
        Spaghetti 127
    Risotto with Asparagus, Tomato,
        and Sage 131
    Stuffed Tomatoes, Patio 125
    Tomato-Fennel Soup 49
    Tomato Pudding Tallyho 125

Tortilla Medley 117

# V

VEAL
    Veal Italiano 81
    Veal Paprikás 81
    Veal Parmesan Roast 82
    Veal Piccata 80

VEGETABLE DISHES
    see also LEGUMES;
        specific vegetables
    Autumn Leaves 119
    Beef-Vegetable Stir-Fry 77
    Garden Vichyssoise 50
    Gazpacho, Cranbrook Garden 49
    Ratatouille Pie 161
    Ratatouille Relish 187
    Salad Niçoise 65
    Tortilla Medley 117
    Vegetable-Fruit Pasta Salad 66

Venison Loin with Cherry Sauce 101

VINEGARS
    see COOKING WINES, VINEGARS
        & OILS

# W

Whipped Cream, Lavender 178

# Z

ZUCCHINI
    Orecchiette Pasta with Eggplant,
        Zucchini, and Mushrooms 128
    Spiced Zucchini Bread 37
    Zucchini Sausage Pie 158

Let us be nice; let's not be rude

But thank the Lord for all our food.

# CRANBROOK
## REFLECTIONS

**A CULINARY COLLECTION**

The Cranbrook House & Gardens
Auxiliary presents
CRANBROOK REFLECTIONS.
When ordering, please use attached
forms and send $19.95 plus $3.50 for
shipping and handling per address,
payable to
CRANBROOK REFLECTIONS,
and mail to:

CRANBROOK REFLECTIONS
380 Lone Pine Road
Box 801
Bloomfield Hills,
Michigan 48303-0801

---

CRANBROOK REFLECTIONS
380 Lone Pine Road   Box 801
Bloomfield Hills, Michigan
48303-0801

Please send me_____ copies of CRANBROOK REFLECTIONS at $19.95 each.   $_____

Michigan residents add $.80 sales tax each_____

Please gift wrap at $2.00 each_____

Plus postage and handling of $3.50 per address_____

Total $_____

Make checks payable to: CRANBROOK REFLECTIONS
Mail to:

Name_____

Address_____

City_____State_____Zip_____

---

CRANBROOK REFLECTIONS
380 Lone Pine Road   Box 801
Bloomfield Hills, Michigan
48303-0801

Please send me_____ copies of CRANBROOK REFLECTIONS at $19.95 each.   $_____

Michigan residents add $.80 sales tax each_____

Please gift wrap at $2.00 each_____

Plus postage and handling of $3.50 per address_____

Total $_____

Make checks payable to: CRANBROOK REFLECTIONS
Mail to:

Name_____

Address_____

City_____State_____Zip_____

---

CRANBROOK REFLECTIONS
380 Lone Pine Road   Box 801
Bloomfield Hills, Michigan
48303-0801

Please send me_____ copies of CRANBROOK REFLECTIONS at $19.95 each.   $_____

Michigan residents add $.80 sales tax each_____

Please gift wrap at $2.00 each_____

Plus postage and handling of $3.50 per address_____

Total $_____

Make checks payable to: CRANBROOK REFLECTIONS
Mail to:

Name_____

Address_____

City_____State_____Zip_____

**Gift wrap and send to the following:**

Name_____

Address_____

City_____State_____Zip_____

Gift card to read:_____

_____

**Gift wrap and send to the following:**

Name_____

Address_____

City_____State_____Zip_____

Gift card to read:_____

_____

**Gift wrap and send to the following:**

Name_____

Address_____

City_____State_____Zip_____

Gift card to read:_____

_____